Beethoven
The Piano Sonatas

An Anthology of Selected Writings

BEETHOVEN
As depicted by the life mask taken by Franz Klein in 1812
(derived from a copy in the author's possession)

BEETHOVEN
THE PIANO SONATAS

AN ANTHOLOGY OF SELECTED WRITINGS

Terence M. Russell

Jelly Bean Books

The right of Terence Russell to be identified as the Author of the Work has been asserted by him in accordance with the Copyright, Designs and Patents Act 1988.

Copyright © Terence M. Russell 2022

Published by
Jelly Bean Books
136 Newport Road
Cardiff
CF24 1DJ

ISBN: 978-1-915439-08-6

www.candyjarbooks.co.uk

All rights reserved.
No part of this publication may be reproduced, stored in a retrieval system, or transmitted at any time or by any means, electronic, mechanical, photocopying, recording or otherwise without the prior permission of the copyright holder. This book is sold subject to the condition that it shall not by way of trade or otherwise be circulated without the publisher's prior consent in any form of binding or cover other than that in which it is published.

CONTENTS

Author's Note	I
Introduction	IX
Editorial Principles	XV
Beethoven's Financial Transactions	XVII

Beethoven: The Piano Sonatas – An Anthology
of Selected Writings:

Allgemeine musikalische Zeitung (AmZ)	2
George Antheil	7
Claudio Arrau	8
Daniel Barenboim	10
Philip Barford	11
Béla Bartók	12
Paul Bekker	12
Hector Berlioz	13
Arthur Bliss	16
Ernst Bloch	17

Eric Blom	18
Alfred Brendel	19
Benjamin Britten	22
Hans von Bülow	23
Ferruccio Busoni	24
Elliott Carter	26
John V. Cockshot	27
Martin Cooper	27
Carl Czerny	28
Carl Dahlhaus	33
Claude Debussy	34
Antonín Dvorák	34
George Dyson	35
Alfred Einstein	36
Ernst von Elterlein	37
Dorothea von Ertmann	40
Brian Ferneyhough	42
Edwin Fischer	43
Leopold Godowsky	47
Stewart Gordon	48
Percy Grainger	49
Sir Charles Hallé	50
E. T. A. Hoffman	53
Vincent D'Indy	54
William Kinderman	56
H. C. Robbins Landon	57
Theodor Leschetizky	57
Franz Liszt	58
Witold Lutoslovwski	68
Edward MacDowell	69
Gustav Mahler	70
Dennis Matthews	70
Wilfrid Mellers	74
Olivier Messian	74

William S. Newman	75
Carl Nielsen	75
Sir Hubert Parry	76
Menahan Pressler	78
Sergei Prokofiev	79
Sviatoslav Richter	81
Ferdinand Ries	82
Romain Rolland	86
Charles Rosen	87
Anton Rubinstein	92
Arthur Rubinstein	95
Sir John Russell	97
Matthew Rye	98
Camille Saint-Saëns	98
Anton Felix Schindler	100
Artur Schnabel	106
Arnold Schoenberg	115
Harold Charles Schonberg	115
Clara Schumann	117
Alexander Scriabin	120
Peter Serkin	121
John Shedlock	121
John Sloboda	123
Leopold Stokowski	124
Igor Stravinsky	124
Peter Tchaikovsky	126
Alexander Wheelock Thayer	127
Virgil Thomson	129
Donald Francis Tovey	130
Richard Wagner	132
Anton von Webern	134
Hugo Wolf	136
BIBLIOGRAPHY	139

INDEX	175
ABOUT THE AUTHOR	177

AUTHOR'S NOTE

I have cherished the idea of making a study of the life and work of Beethoven for many years. This statement requires a few words of personal reflection. I first encountered Beethoven in my early piano lessons — Minuet in G major, WoO 10, No. 2. At the same time I became acquainted with his piano pupil Carl Czerny — *Book One, Piano Studies*. My heart sank when I discovered the rear cover advertised a further *99* books in the same series — scales, arpeggios studies for the left hand, studies for the right hand — all the way to his Op. 824! By coincidence, my *Czerny Book One* was edited by Alec Rowley — who had the same surname as my music teacher. In my childish innocence, I often wondered why *he himself* never appeared to give me a lesson!

In my teenage years I found myself drawn ever closer to Beethoven's music in the manner that ferromagnetic materials are ineluctably held captive in the sway of a magnetic field. The impulse to which I yielded is well described in words the conductor Bruno Walter gave in one of his rare public addresses: 'It is my belief that young people at that age are more easily impressed by what is heroic and grandiose; that they more easily understand works of art in which passionate feelings are violently uttered in raised accents, and that the lighter sounds of cheerfulness are less impressive to them.' I do indeed recall the stirring effect made on me on first hearing the Overture *Egmont*, the unfolding drama of the Fifth Symphony and the declamatory opening chords of the *Emperor* Piano Concerto.

I resolved to read everything I could about Beethoven, starting with Marion Scott's pioneering English-language study of the composer in the *Master Musicians series*. My father took out a subscription for me for *The Gramophone* magazine, enabling me to read reviews of the new 'LP' recordings — none of which though I could afford! The LP was then — 1950s — beginning to supplant the 78 rpm shellac records, stacks of which could be purchased for as little as six pence each in 'old' money. At this same time I had the privilege of hearing Beethoven's music performed by the *Hallé Orchestra* under the baton of Sir John Barbirolli, and experienced the *Carl Rosa Opera Company* perform the composer's only opera *Fidelio*; I borrowed the piano-reduction score from the City Library to become better acquainted with this moving work — only to find the score's fists full of notes were well beyond my capabilities. Nonetheless, since then *Fidelio's* every note has been woven into my DNA. I also recall the period when the *London Promenade Concerts* were designated 'Friday night is Beethoven night'.

Through these influences I resolved to visit Vienna to see where Beethoven had lived and worked. But how? The support for such travel was beyond the means of my family. Fortunately in my final year at school (1959) an opportunity presented itself. I saw a poster that stated *WUS – World University Service* – required volunteers to work in the Austrian town of Linz to help relocate refugees who were living there in improvised wooden shacks – displaced and dispossessed victims of the Second World War. To those participating all expenses would be paid together with free accommodation – in one of the crumbling wooden shacks! From Linz, I planned to make my way to Vienna.

I applied to *WUS* and, despite being a mere school-leaver, I was accepted. The *WUS* authorities doubtless reasoned the building-trade skills I had acquired during my secondary education in the building department of a technical school would be useful. This proved to be the case. At the refugee camp I dug trenches and was allowed to assist as a bricklayer. All about me were wide-eyed children eager to help but mostly getting in the way. I recall one afternoon when a reporter from *The Observer* newspaper paid a visit to our construction site to gather material for an article he was writing on European post-war recovery – he generously admired my trenches and brickwork!

Of lasting significance was another visit, this time from a Belgian priest. He took a group of us to the nearby *Mauthausen* Concentration Camp, recently opened as a silent and solemn memorial to those who had perished there. It was a deeply moving experience. Years later I learned of the views of the ardent Beethovenian Sir Michael Tippet. After the horrors of the *Holocaust,* he posed the question for mankind: 'What price Beethoven now?' He posited: 'Could we any longer find solace in Beethoven's setting of Schiller's *Ode to Joy* and its utopian vision – "Be embraced you Millions"?'

My refugee contribution duly came to end and Vienna beckoned. On arrival there I found scenes reminiscent of *The Third Man* and *Harry Lime*. I recall, for example, encountering cobblestones piled high in the streets waiting to be replaced after having been disturbed by the heavy armoured vehicles that had so recently passed over them. But Vienna was welcoming. I visited the houses where Beethoven had lived and worked and paused outside others associated with him that were identified by a commemorative plaque and the Austrian flag. A particularly memorable occasion was attending a recital in the great salon within the palace of Beethoven's noble patron Prince Lobkowitz — the very one where the *Eroica* Symphony had been premiered. Ultimately, my steps led me to the composer's first resting place in the *Währinger Ortsfriedhof*. I paid silent homage to the great man and, as I did so, discovered nearby the resting place of Franz Schubert to whom Beethoven was an endless source of admiration and inspiration.

I felt a youthful impulse to discover yet more about Beethoven and his music. But absorption in musicology would have to take second place. My chosen career beckoned in the guise of architecture — 'the mother of the arts' and 'the handmaid of society'. There was room though for Beethoven's music and from that time on it has been my constant companion through attendance at recitals, in concerts and music-making in the home. And at home a reproduction of Franz Kline's 1812 study of the composer has greeted me each day for more than half a century.

On my retirement from a career in architectural practice, research and university teaching, the opportunity finally presented itself for me to devote time to researching Beethoven musicology. Having attained my eightieth year also emboldened me to make progress with my good intentions!

With these autobiographical remarks outlined I will say a few remarks about my working method — see also the comments made in *Editorial Principles*.

As a member of staff of The University of Edinburgh, I had the good fortune to have access to the *Reid Music Library*, formed from a nucleus of books bequeathed by General John Reid and augmented over the years by such custodians as Sir Donald Francis Tovey, sometime *Reid Professor of Music* and renowned Beethoven scholar. Over a period of three years, I made a survey of the many works in the Reid collection. I consulted each item in turn making records on paper slips — many hundreds — that I deemed to be relevant for my researches. I confined my searches to book-publications, as reflected in my accompanying bibliography. All of this was quite some years ago, the cut-off date for my researches being 2007. Beyond this date I have not surveyed any further works. I am mindful though that Beethoven musicology and related publication continue to be a major field of endeavour in the manner of the proverbial 'ever rolling stream'.

In the intervening years since completing my archival researches, personal tribulations associated with family illness and bereavement slowed my progress in giving expression to my projected intentions. Latterly, however, with renewed energy, and more time at my disposal, I have been able to make progress. My studies take the form of a set of monographs. These trace the creation origins and reception history of each of Beethoven's piano sonatas and string quartets. The resulting texts also incorporate contextual accounts of Beethoven and his contemporaries. Also included in my musicological surveys are two related Beethoven anthologies. The set of monographs in question, identified by short title, are:

Beethoven: An anthology of selected writings.
Beethoven: The piano sonatas: An anthology of selected writings.

The Piano Sonatas:
Op. 2–Op. 28
Op. 31–Op. 81A
Op. 90–Op. 111

The String Quartets:
Op. 18, Nos. 1–6
Op. 59, Nos. 1–3 (Razumovsky); Op. 74 (The Harp);
 Op. 95 (Quartetto Serioso)
Op. 127, Op. 132 and Op. 130 (Galitzin)
Op. 131, Op. 135; Grosse Fuge, Op. 133 and Op. 134
 (Fugue transcription)

I provide further information about these studies in the introduction to each individual monograph. Suffice it for me to state here the basic premise upon which my work is founded. I believe it is rewarding, concerning the life of a great artist, to find connections between who he *was* and what he *did*; in Martin Cooper's words 'between his personality, as expressed on the one hand in human relationships, and on the other in artistic creation'. (*Beethoven, The Last Decade*) That is not to say I consider it essential to the enjoyment of Beethoven's music to know this or that fact about it. His music can be enjoyed, as millions do, with — in Robert Simpson's apt phrase —'an innocent ear', for what it is and how it reaches out to us in purely musical terms without any prejudging of its merits based upon extra-musicological facts.

I must make a further point. I am mindful that a scholar who ventures into a field of study that is not rightly his may be regarded with some suspicion. In this regard I can but ask the reader to place his or her trust in me in the following way. I have attempted to bring to my work the care which publishers and their desk editors have required of me in my book writings relating to architecture — listed elsewhere.

As inferred, it is now more than sixty years since I paid homage to Beethoven in Vienna's *Währinger Ortsfriedhof* and my warmth of feeling towards the composer and his music have grown with the passing of the years. My studies are not intended to be propaedeutic — that would be pretentious. However, if in sharing with others what I have to say contributes to their knowledge and understanding of the composer, and thereby increases their own feelings towards him and his works, my own pleasure in bringing my work to completion will be all the more enhanced.

It is perhaps fitting that my studies should appear in Beethoven's 250th Anniversary Year — I must confess more by chance than design!

When Beethoven arrived in Vienna, he was unknown. He was armed though with a note of encouragement from his youthful friend and benefactor Count Ferdinand Waldstein. It contained the often-quoted words: 'Receive Mozart's spirit from Haydn's hands.' Some forty years later Beethoven passed away in the House of the black-robed Spaniards at 200 *Alservorstädter*, the *Glacis* where he had lived since the autumn of 1825. Soldiers had to be called to secure the doors to the inner courtyard of the house from the pressure of onlookers. His body was blessed in the *Alservorsttädt Parish Church*, schools were closed and perhaps as many as 10,000 people formed a funeral procession — an honour ordinarily reserved for monarchs. The *Marcia Funebre* from the composer's Op. 26 Piano Sonata was performed at the funeral ceremony. Franz Grillparzer read the funeral oration. Franz Schubert, who, as remarked in life so admired Beethoven, was one of the pallbearers. The composer's mortal remains were lowered into a simple vault. Beethoven now belonged to history.

Dr Terence M. Russell
Edinburgh 2020

INTRODUCTION

As the title to this anthology implies, it consists of a compilation of texts that bring together views bearing on the piano sonatas of Ludwig van Beethoven. As such it provides a collective estimation of his achievement in this genre as expressed through the sayings and writings of fellow musicians, musicologists and performing artists. In selecting the texts for inclusion, my primary intention has been to make available to the reader the opinions of recognised authorities bearing on such considerations as the composer's aesthetic and creative impulses; his philosophical and intellectual outlook; the expressive nature of his writing for the piano; the pianistic challenges he sets the performer relating to questions of interpretation and performance; and, most notably, the continuing legacy of his musical inheritance in the genre of the piano sonata. Where applicable, prefatory remarks to the selected texts are incorporated in order to provide the reader with the original context from which the various writings have been derived. With this in mind, the bibliographical references that identify the origins of the various texts and quotations are also identified. The bibliography at the close of the work will also be of value to the reader wishing to discover more about the original sources and others not specifically cited in the main text. In this context, mention should be made of the author's three companion studies that survey the creation origins and reception history of Beethoven's thirty-two piano sonatas. These are:

Beethoven: The piano sonatas: Op. 2–Op. 28: Their creation origins and reception history

Beethoven: The piano sonatas: Op. 31–Op. 79: Their creation origins and reception history

Beethoven: The piano sonatas: Op. 90–Op. 111: Their creation origins and reception history

These individual monographs contain many citations to Beethoven and his works and to remarks made about them. Concerning Beethoven, in the wider context of his legacy to cultural history, the reader may wish to consult the author's further companion study, *Beethoven: An anthology of selected writings.*

The virtues of Beethoven's piano sonatas have been recognised from the period of their inception. In 1800, when the composer was becoming established in Vienna, a reviewer writing of his most recent compositions for the keyboard, published in the influential *Allgemeine musikalische Zeitung*, was disposed to remark: 'Herr Beethoven [is] a man of genius ... with ... originality ... possessing an abundance of ideas [and who] goes entirely his own way.' Towards the end of Beethoven's life, a music critic writing in the pages of the same journal reflected: 'The composer struck along new paths some thirty years ago.' He acknowledged his works had 'engendered hostility on the way' but conceded 'all that is now stilled for today no other can touch this great spirit'. Anton Felix Schindler, Beethoven's secretary-assistant and early biographer, likened the piano sonatas to 'portraits of the heart'. Typical of his effusive style, and the manner of endorsement of his master's work, he continues: 'Consider the form of the first movement of the first Sonata in F minor, how different it is from the form of the first movement of the Sonata in E-flat major, Op. 7! And how different again are the first movements of the Sonata in C minor Op. 10 and the *Pathétique* Op. 13, and so on through the wonderfully inspired Sonatas Op. 57 (F minor), Op. 90 (E minor), right up to the last!'

As evidence of their centrality to European culture, the nineteenth-century pianist and conductor Hans von Bülow likened the forty-eight preludes and fugues of Bach to the *Old Testament* and the thirty-two piano sonatas of Beethoven to the *New Testament*. Richard Wagner, in his extensive prose works, considered Beethoven's piano sonatas to be 'a veil through which he looked into the realm of tones' and 'through which he spoke to us from out that realm'. Throughout the nineteenth century, ever widening audiences became aware of these compositions and likewise more virtuosi were able to perform them. In his *Beethoven piano sonatas* of 1875, (English edition 1898), the influential German musicologist Ernst von Elterlein felt able to write: 'The transcendental beauty and the exceeding importance of Beethoven's pianoforte sonatas are facts now universally recognised ... and various nations now emulate each other's efforts in issuing correct and excellent editions of these great works ... Thus will Beethoven's music extend into an ever-widening circle, and the temple of true musical beauty will be more widely opened and become a greater blessing to mankind.'

The fiercely impassioned Beethovenian Hector Berlioz remarked: 'In these piano works the performer's task is made overwhelming, not so much by the technical difficulties as by the deep feeling and the musical intelligence that the works demand. Antonin Dvorák confessed: 'How much time I spent learning the rich forms of Beethoven's sonatas' and, after a lifetime of study and performance of the these works, the French philosopher, dramatist and musicologist Romain Rolland pronounced Beethoven to be 'the universal musician above all others'. On the occasion of Beethoven's Death Centenary (1927), the British composer and pioneering musical educationalist Sir George Dyson wrote: 'When the heat of his passion demands the impossible, it is because his vision is of things beyond man's power to describe. In pursuit of that transcendence, Beethoven spent himself. And if his fire sometimes scorches us it consumed his ardent soul no less.'

The Austrian pianist Artur Schnabel was the first to record the complete cycle of Beethoven's thirty-two sonatas and also published a meticulously edited performing edition. Comparing composers he once stated: 'Mozart is a garden, Schubert is a forest of light and shade, but Beethoven is a mountain range.' Ernst Bloch believed 'passion, pain cheerfulness and liberation' to be the authentic and encompassing components of a Beethoven sonata. Edward MacDowell considered Beethoven invested instrumental music, including the piano sonatas, 'with a wonderful poignancy and power of expression, elevating it to the point of being the medium of expressing some of the greatest thoughts we posses'. In his estimation of Beethoven's achievement, musicologist Paul Bekker recognized that when at the height of his powers — before the onset of deafness — Beethoven had been one of the foremost keyboard virtuosi of his day remarking: 'In the pianoforte sonatas we posses an absolutely subjective confession of faith from a practising artist.' In his appreciation of Beethoven's piano sonatas, William Kinderman combines the insights of a performing artist with those of an acknowledged Beethoven authority: 'The influence of these works has been incalculable and has left an imprint not only on subsequent compositions and performance traditions but also on the development of serious musical criticism and analysis shaping the very ways in which we think about musical art.'

Ernst Theodor Amadeus Hoffman was among the first of Beethoven's contemporaries to write discerning reviews of his compositions. Discussing the interpretation of the composer's music he stated: 'Beethoven asks nothing more than that one should understand him, that one should enter deeply into his being, that — conscious of one's own consecration — one should boldly dare to step inside the circle of the magical phenomena that his powerful spell has evoked.' A century later, Donald Francis Tovey, the doyen among Beethoven musicologists of his generation, said much the same thing: 'Trust Beethoven, play what he tells you and train your ear to what you play.' In the 1920s, the Swiss pianist Edwin Fischer addressed a group of students on the subject of interpretation — as posed by Beethoven's sonatas. He enthused: 'What delight and happiness [Beethoven] offered the player! ... He must puzzle out, be an actor, exchange the orchestra for the organ, be a pianist, singer, string player — all in one!' Fischer's sometime pupil, and respected interpreter of Beethoven, Alfred Brendel considers Beethoven's piano sonatas to be part of the pianist's 'daily bread' and of their realization has said:

'Playing his thirty-two piano sonatas is so satisfying because taken as a whole they are all necessary, at least as contrasts to each other.' This remark calls to mind Beethoven's assertion that 'he never repeated himself'.

We draw these introductory remarks to a close with observations from Beethoven's precociously gifted pupil Carl Czerny who learned many of the piano sonatas directly under the composer's guidance. In his notes on *The proper performance of Beethoven's works for the piano*, he encourages the would-be student of these compositions to follow the time-honoured advice: 'Maintain the correct tempo; observe all expression marks; and thoroughly master all technical difficulties for the cultivation of a good execution.'

We give the last word here to the musicologist Eric Blom. In his *Beethoven's pianoforte sonatas discussed* he writes: 'Their greatness has softened the composer's asperities and rudenesses and made them for us, over and above their purely musical wonders, into an intensely individual expression of the most irresistible fascination. We still live with his sonatas, and the world will go on doing so as it has such civilization of the mind to keep in spite of its failure to attain to that universal brotherhood of mankind that was Beethoven's delusion.'

TMR

EDITORIAL PRINCIPLES

By its very nature a study of this kind draws extensively on the work of others. Every effort has been made to acknowledge this in the text by indicating words quoted or adapted with single quotation marks. Wherever possible, for the sake of consistency, I have retained the orthography of quoted texts making only occasional silent changes of spelling and capitalization. Deleted words are identified by means of three ellipsis points ... and interpolations are encompassed within square brackets [ ]. Quoted words, phrases and longer cited passages of text remain the intellectual property of their copyright holders.

I address the reader in the second person notwithstanding that the work is my own. It follows that I must bear the responsibility for any errors of misunderstanding or misinterpretation for which I ask the reader's forbearance. A collaboration I must acknowledge is the help I received from the librarians of the Reid Music Library at the University of Edinburgh. Over the three-year period it took me to compile my reference sources, they served me with unfailing courtesy, often supplying me with twenty or more books at a time. In converting my manuscript into book format, I wish to thank my editorial coordinator, William Rees, for his support and painstaking care. I would also like to thank Shaun Russell for his work designing the cover for each of the twelve volumes.

My admiration for Beethoven provided the initial impulse to commence this undertaking and has sustained me over the several years it has taken to bring my enterprise to completion. That said, I am no Beethoven idolater. I am mindful of the danger that awaits one who ventures to chronicle the work of a great artist. I believe it was Sigmund Freud who suggested that biographers may become so disposed to their subject, and their emotional involvement with their hero, that their work becomes an exercise in idealisation. In response to such a charge let me say. First, I am no biographer. I do however make occasional reference to Beethoven's personal life and his relationships with his contemporaries. Second, I acknowledge Beethoven has his detractors. Accordingly, I have not shrunk from allowing dissentient voices, critical of Beethoven and his work, to be heard. These, however, are few and are silenced amidst the adulation that awaits the reader in support of the endeavours of one of humanity's great creators and one who courageously showed the way in overcoming personal adversity.

TMR

BEETHOVEN'S FINANCIAL TRANSACTIONS

Beethoven's negotiations with his music publishers make many references to his compositions. Today they are recognised for what they are – enduring works of art – but referred to in his business correspondence they appear almost as though they were mere everyday commodities – for which he required an appropriate remuneration. Beethoven resented the time he had to devote to the business-side of his affairs. He believed an agency should exist, for fellow artists such as himself, from which a reasonable sum could be paid for the work (composition) submitted, leaving more time for creative enterprises. In the event Beethoven, like Mozart before him, had to deal with publishers largely on his own. Beethoven, though, did benefit in his business dealings from the help he received from his younger brother Kasper Karl (Caspar Carl). From

1800, Carl worked as a clerk in Vienna's Department of Finance in which capacity he found time to correspond with publishers to offer his brother's works for sale and — importantly — to secure the best prices he could. In April 1802 Beethoven wrote to the Leipzig publishers Breitkopf & Härtel: '[You] can rely entirely on my brother who, in general, attends to my affairs.' Whilst Carl promoted Beethoven's interests with determination, he appears to have lacked tact and made enemies. For example, Beethoven's piano pupil Ferdinand Ries — who for a while also helped the composer with his business negotiations — is on record as describing Carl as being 'the biggest skinflint in the world'. The currencies most referred to in Beethoven's correspondence are as follows:

> silver gulden and florin: these were interchangeable and had a value of about two English/British shillings
> ducat: 4 1/2 gulden/florins: valued at about nine shillings
> louis d'or: This gold coin was adopted during the Napoleonic wars and the French occupation of Vienna and Austria more widely. It had a value of about two ducats or approximately twenty shillings or one-pound sterling.

Beethoven was never poor — in the romantic sense of 'an artist starving in a garret'. On arriving in Vienna in 1792, he was fortunate to receive financial support from his patron Prince Karl Lichnowsky who conferred on him an annuity of 600 florins that he maintained for several years. Between the months of February and July of 1796, Beethoven undertook a concert tour taking in Prague, Dresden, Leipzig and Berlin. He was well received and wrote to his other younger brother Nikolaus Johann: 'My art is winning me friends and what more do I want? ... I shall make a good deal of money.' Later on, in 1809, Napoleon Bonaparte's youngest brother Jérôme Bonaparte offered Beethoven an appointment at his Court with the promise of an income of 4,000 florins. Alarmed at the prospect of losing Beethoven — now the most celebrated composer in Europe — three of Vienna's most notable citizens, namely, the Archduke Rudolph (Beethoven's only composition pupil), Prince Kinsky and Prince Lobkowitz settled on the composer the same sum of 4,000 florins. Inflation, however, brought about by the Napoleonic wars, soon eroded its value; personal misfortune to Lobkowitz and Kinsky also took its toll.

Beethoven undoubtedly had to work hard to secure a reasonable standard of living. Notwithstanding, despite his occasional straitened circumstances, he contributed generously to the needs of others. For example, he allowed his works to be performed free of charge at charitable concerts; in 1815 his philanthropy earned for him the honour of Bürgerrecht — 'freedom of the City'.

Beethoven earned a great deal of money when his music was performed, to considerable acclaim, at several concerts held in association with the Congress of Vienna (1814-15). He did not though benefit from it personally; he invested it on behalf of his nephew Karl. It is one of the misfortunes of Beethoven's life that in money-matters he was culpably improvident. This is poignantly evident in a letter he wrote on 18 March 1827 to the Philharmonic Society of London just one week before his death; the Society had made him a gift of £100. He sent the Society 'his most heartfelt thanks for their particular sympathy and support'.

TMR

The marvellous thing about Beethoven's sonatas is that they are so different, each of them... Beethoven the man had his limitations and frailties, but as a composer he encompassed and mastered nearly everything that is human. And of course the last sonata is an essence of this humanity; it is a true conclusion of the series.

Alfred Brendel in conversation with David Dubal
in: Dubal, David, *The world of the concert pianist*,
London: Victor Gollancz, 1985.

SELECTED WRITINGS

This study consists of a compilation of writings bearing on Beethoven's achievements in the genre of the piano sonata. They are illustrative of views expressed about these compositions, as conveyed through the sayings and writings of musicians, musicologists and performing artists. As such they provide insights into such considerations as the composer's aesthetic and creative impulse; his philosophical and intellectual outlook; the expressive nature of his writing; the challenges with which he confronts the performer relating to questions of interpretation and performance; and, above all, the continuing legacy of his musical inheritance

Where applicable, prefatory remarks are incorporated with the selected texts to provide the reader with the original context from which the various writings have been derived. The bibliography at the close of the work will also be of value to the reader wishing to discover more about the original sources and others publications not cited in the selected texts.

ALLGEMEINE MUSIKALISCHE ZEITUNG (AmZ)

The *Allgemeine musikalische Zeitung* (*General music Newspaper*) was a German-language periodical that commenced publication in 1798 under the direction of its owner and founder Gottfried Christoph Härtel. Its publisher was Breitkopf & Härtel of Leipzig with whom Beethoven had many negotiations. The periodical reviewed musical events taking place in the German-speaking nations and in other countries. As such, it was amongst the first to bring to the attention of the musically minded public an awareness of Beethoven's compositions and of their originality — that the periodical's contributors frequently found to be disturbing.

In 1800, the *AmZ* published a review ostensibly in celebration of Joseph Haydn to whom it accorded 'the first place' with regard to his symphonies and quartets, 'wherein no one has yet surpassed him'.

Beethoven, a still relatively unknown composer, is not however overlooked; the reviewer comments how he may even usurp the venerable master 'if he calms his wild imaginings'.

With the publication of the Piano Sonatas Op. 10 Nos. 1–3 the *AmZ* reviewer recognised:

> 'Herr Beethoven [for being] a man of genius ...
> with ... originality ... possessing an abundance of
> ideas [and who] goes entirely his own way'.

For the critic in question though, it appears Beethoven went a little too far. The composer is censured on the grounds his gift 'too often causes him to pile up ideas without restraint and to arrange them by means of a bizarre order'.

He does, however, conclude with a compliment, albeit a somewhat backhanded one:

'There are undoubtedly few artists to whom one must exclaim: save up your treasures and be thrifty with them.'

The issue of the *AmZ* for 19 February 1800 included a review of Beethoven's Piano Sonata Op. 13, *The Pathétique*. The reviewer was probably Johann Rochlitz, a founder contributor of the *Allgemeine musikalische Zeitung* and a fervent admirer of Beethoven – although some of his later reviews earned Beethoven's occasional irony and critical displeasure. Rochlitz perceptively describes the work as having 'a definitely passionate character' and being 'noble and melancholy'. He found 'pathos' and 'earnest passion' to permeate the mood of the first movement augmented by 'strong determination'. Although then only a young man, Beethoven is praised for his 'impressive command of tragic expression' and for 'an attitude of resistance' 'even defiance' His music, Rochlitz observes, has 'concentrated power' and is 'loaded with dark pathos'

The review concludes:

'It must be a pleasant feeling for the Viennese music public ... to have so many excellent artists. [Herr] van Beethoven unquestionably belongs to them.'

The review of Beethoven's Piano Sonatas Op. 26 and Op. 27, in the June 1802 issue of the *AmZ*, contained an observation with which many pianists, professional and amateur alike will, at some time, doubtless have felt a sense of identity:

> '[The] reviewer does not complain about difficulties of execution when they are necessary for the representation of a significant idea ... However, [Herr] v. Beethoven should not so often expect the admirers of his compositions to play movements that can only be played properly with an extraordinarily large hand.'

Turning to the musical merits of the works in question, the reviewer concluded:

> 'These are the three piano compositions with which Herr v[an]. B[eethoven] recently enriched a selected few cultivated musicians and accomplished pianists. I say enriched, because they are truly an enrichment and belong among those few works of art of the present day that will scarcely ever grow old; certainly number three [*The Moonlight*] can never grow old.'

Of this Sonata he enthused:

> 'This *Fantasia* is one solid whole from beginning to end; it arises all at once from an undivided, profound, and intimately excited heart and is cut, as it were, from one block of marble.'

The reviewer also hints at the technical challenges posed by the compositions:

> 'Less educated musicians, and those who expect nothing more from music than a facile entertainment, will pick up these works in vain.'

Four months after publication of the Piano Sonata Op. 28, the work was reviewed in the 8 December Issue of the *AmZ*. By now Beethoven's reputation for daring and innovation were beginning to earn the reviewer's respect:

> 'Beethoven remains faithful to his character and manner ... an artist like B[eethoven] can really do nothing better than remain faithful to himself.'

Of the music, the reviewer adds:

> '[Op. 28] is on a very large scale and is peculiar to the extent of being strange and adventurous, particularly the first and third movements.'

On 26 January 1806, a review of the *Waldstein* Piano Sonata duly appeared in the *Allgemeine musikalische Zeitung*. The reviewer praised the work's first and last movements for being 'amongst the most brilliant and original pieces for which we are grateful to this master' but, he added, 'they are also full of strange whims and are very difficult to perform'.

Twenty years later (10 May 1826), a review of a four-hand arrangement of the Piano Sonata was published by the AmZ's sister journal the Berliner *Allgemeine musikalische Zeitung*. This is of interest for its opening remarks. They shed light on the extent to which the music fraternity had by then adopted the *Waldstein Sonata* since its publication. The reviewer enthuses:

> This magnificent work has long been well known to all keyboard players, with its original power, loftiness, and loveliness of the first movement, the breath of spring of its second movement, which comes smilingly forth as though from the regions of the soul.'

When the Piano Sonata Op. 57 was published, this circumstance was not lost on the music critic assigned to review the work in the *AmZ*. Mindful that the composition could not be fully realized on the older-style instruments, with their more restricted keyboard, he observes:

> '[This] entire sonata extends the range of the pianoforte, and very frequently, up to three octaves above middle C, without the passages that go above the G below being transcribed, or being very easy to transcribe.'

In due course the *Allgemeine musikalische Zeitung* received news of Beethoven's compositions with increased respect. A music critic writing in issue XXVI of the *AmZ* of 1824 made a survey of Beethoven's pianos sonatas in what would be its longest contemporary review of these piano compositions. He enthuses: 'The composer struck along new paths some thirty years ago.' He acknowledges his works 'engendered hostility on the way' but concedes 'all that is now stilled for today no other can touch this great spirit'. In particular, he praises 'the structure, melody, harmony, and rhythm' of the last three Sonatas (Opp. 109, 110 and 111). Whilst acknowledging their 'many technical difficulties' he reassures the would-be performer that 'non of these is insurmountable'.

Wayne M. Senner, Robin Wallace and William Meredith, editors, *The critical reception of Beethoven's compositions by his German contemporaries*. Lincoln: University of Nebraska Press, in association with the American Beethoven Society and the Ira F. Brilliant Center for Beethoven Studies, San José State University, 1999: Vol. 1, p. 147, pp. 176–7 and pp. 180–1; and Vol. 2, pp. 45–8. See also: H. C. Robbins Landon, *Haydn: The Years of the Creation*. London: Thames and Hudson, 1977, p. 590. Many other reviews from the *AmZ* are cited in Anton Felix Schindler, *Beethoven as I Knew Him*, edited by Donald W. MacArdle and translated by Constance S. Jolly from the German edition of 1860, London: Faber and Faber, 1966.

GEORGE ANTHEIL

The American avant-garde composer and pianist, George Antheil, performed a Beethoven piano sonata (he does not say which) at a concert in Leipzig to an audience of Beethoven cognoscente. He concludes his spirited account with the following observation:

> 'What a master Beethoven is! How wonderful he develops, expands his material! How wonderful his harmonic scheme! My GOD, I wonder if I shall ever be able to write music one-tenth as good as this? Alas, probably never. Still I shall try ... These were my thoughts that evening during the *allegro* of the Beethoven sonata ... The public applauded ... Amidst this hysteria I bowed and bowed and thought, What a hell of a way for a man to make a living!'

George Antheil, *Bad Boy of Music. London:* New York: Hurst & Blackett Ltd., 1945. pp. 60–1.

CLAUDIO ARRAU

The Chilean pianist Claudio Arrau was celebrated for his interpretations of a large repertoire including the works of Beethoven, Schubert, Chopin, Schumann, Liszt and Brahms. In 1938 Arrau gave the first rendering of the complete Beethoven piano sonatas and piano concertos in Mexico City. He repeated this feat several times in his lifetime, including in New York and London. He is remembered for being one of the leading Beethoven keyboard authorities of the 20th century. As a tribute to his accomplishments, New York City conferred on him its Beethoven Medal.

When in conversation with the American cultural historian Joseph Horowitz, Arrau expressed his high regard for Beethoven, to the interpretation of whose works he had dedicated so much of his life:

> 'For me, Beethoven has always stood for the spirit of man victorious. His message of endless struggle concluding in the victory of renewal and spiritual rebirth speaks to us and to young people today with a force that is particularly relevant to our times. In the sense that his life was an existential fight for survival, Beethoven is our contemporary. In the sense that he mastered both his life and his art to reach the ultimate heights of creation and transfiguration, he will last as long as man's spirit to prevail lasts on earth.'

Turning to the piano sonatas, Horowitz discussed the question of metronome indications as a guide to performance. In particular he cited the case of the *Hammerklavier* Sonata for which the composer's suggested metronome settings are today considered to demand too fast a tempo.

Arrau responded:

> 'If you play the first movement of the *Hammerklavier* at the metronome tempo, it loses all its majesty.'

He revealed he had tried to perform it at Beethoven's metronome tempo but, although he considered it 'feasible' he personally found it to be 'very difficult technically ... Almost impossible'. He thought Carl Czerny's metronome markings for the sonata deserved respect for being

> 'the only markings from somebody who actually studied with Beethoven and performed under his influence'.

Of these though he accepted — 'they're not too reliable either'. In response to Horowitz's generalization: 'Do you think there is such a thing as a proper tempo for a given piece?' Arrau averred, somewhat laconically: 'There is a proper range, I think. A rather narrow range.'

Horowitz also asked Arrau what his position was concerning the redistribution of notes between the hands in performance to facilitate evenness or accuracy. Arrau acknowledged that an audience may not notice such things but he maintained, 'one should play for the *ideal* listener'.

He believed the ideal listener will notice the difference, and cited passages in the first movement of Op 111:

> 'People play it with two hands because they don't want to risk dirty octaves. Well, first of all, it sounds different played with one hand, as written. And then technical difficulty has itself an expressive value.'

*

On another occasion, in the 1970s, the pianist Philip Lorenz assisted Arrau to conduct a series of master classes; these were in connection with the Beethoven Bicentennial. It was a first-time experience for Arrau. Students attended from, Europe, Japan and America. One student elected to perform the Op. 111 Piano Sonata. Lorenz recalls how, in guiding the pupil, Arrau did not play a single note. Instead he encouraged her with his views about the composition, remarking on 'the emotional world the music occupies and how to realise the work's technical challenges'.

At the close of the student's performance there was thunderous applause. Lorenz remembers:

> 'I think a lot of people were moved to tears ... it wasn't so much for her playing, although she played very well. It was for [Arrau].'

Joseph Horowitz, *Conversations with Arrau*. London: Collins, 1982, p. 21, p. 170 and pp. 214–5.

DANIEL BARENBOIM

The Argentine-Israeli born pianist and conductor Daniel Barenboim was described by Wilhelm Furtwängler as a 'phenomenon' and, whilst only a child, invited him to perform Beethoven's First Piano Concerto. Still only in his teens, Barenboim went on to record the complete series of the composer's piano sonatas. Barenboim is known to be opposed to the practice of choosing the tempo of a piece based on historical evidence, such as the composer's metronome marks — considered by some to be unreliable in Beethoven's scores. Instead, he prefers to find the correct tempo from within the music itself. Barenboim makes the following remarks concerning interpretation in music:

> 'Every masterpiece is open to any number of interpretations, as long as they do not falsify it. However, it is not possible to combine all interpretations in any one performance, just as it is impossible to live more than one life. The interpreter or the performer can never perceive all the many details of the many possible interpretations in any one performance, he can only glimpse them. We often become obsessed with one particular viewpoint or idea, and thus become blind to its opposite. But to me, dualism, the paradoxical nature of things, is the very essence of music. It is no coincidence that the sonata form, which is based on this dualism, is one of the most perfect forms of expression. The structure of a classical sonata or symphony by Beethoven is based on this principal of dualism.'

Daniel Barenboim, *A Life in Music*. London: Weidenfeld & Nicolson, 1991, p. 209.

PHILIP BARFORD

The musicologist and author Philip Barford discuses *unity* in musical form:

> 'The essential inspiration is always unity — unity as experience, unity as idea, unity as a system of interrelated parts, unity as contrast, unity as an invisible world-spirit manifesting itself in the transformation of organic forms and the transmutation of life-energies through perception, imagi-

nation, thought and intuition. Beethoven knew
unity through discovery of the formative forces
locked up in musical shapes.'

Philip Barford, [*Beethoven*]: *The Piano Music* (II) in: Denis Arnold and Nigel Fortune, editors, *The Beethoven Companion*. London: Faber and Faber, 1973, p. 193.

BÉLA BARTÓK

Whilst teaching at Harvard University in 1940, Bartók arranged to give piano lessons to his private pupil Dorothy Parrish. She must have been a pianist of considerable talent, given the nature of Bartók's response to her requests for study material:

> 'As for works to study, you may choose whatever you like from all the works of Beethoven (except the last Sonata, and the *Hammerklavier*), by Mozart, Bach Schubert, Chopin, Schumann, Debussy and — Bartók!'

Janos Demény, editor, *Béla Bartók Letters*. London: Faber and Faber, 1971, pp. 279–80.

PAUL BEKKER

The German music critic Paul Bekker considers the aspect of *faith* in Beethoven's art:

> 'It makes no real difference to us whether Beethoven did or did not, as a performer, answer to his own ideal; or whether, in later years, his performance deteriorated on account of his

deafness, or his neglect of the technical side of his art. What matters is the certainty that in the pianoforte works we possess an absolutely subjective confession of faith from a practising artist. They give us a glimpse into his workshop. Through them we get authentic tidings of his wishes and purposes; they form a diary of the deepest, most individual and intimate description.'

Paul Bekker, *Beethoven.* London: J. M. Dent & Sons, 1925, p. 145.

HECTOR BERLIOZ

Hector Berlioz's enthusiasm for the music of Beethoven is well documented. He himself gave expression to it in his *A travers chants, etudes musicales, adorations, boutades et crtiques,* an English edition of which was translated and edited by Edwin Evans and was published in 1911 under the title *A critical study of Beethoven's nine symphonies, with a few words on his trios and sonatas, a criticism of Fidelio and an introductory essay on music,* London, W. Reeves, 1911. More than thirty years after Beethoven's death his works were little known in France. Those that were performed, in particular the orchestral works, were usually premiered in severely edited and truncated form and were typically received with hostility. The symphonies were condemned for being

'bizarre, incoherent, diffuse, bristling with harsh modulations and wild harmonies, bereft of melody, over the top, too noisy, and horribly difficult to play'.

*

Amidst such clamour, the views of Hector Berlioz were an oasis of calm and reason, albeit with more than a touch of Gallic passion. Writing about the piano sonatas, Berlioz remarks:

> 'In these piano works the performer's task is made overwhelming, not so much by the technical difficulties as by the deep feeling and the musical intelligence that the works demand. The virtuoso must absolutely efface himself before the composer, just as the orchestra does in the symphonies. There must be complete absorption of the one by the other; and it is precisely in this identifying himself with the thought he conveys that the performer rises to the greatness of his model.'

Cited by Elizabeth Csicserry-Ronay, translator and editor, Hector Berlioz: *The art of music and other essays*: (*A travers chants*), Bloomington: Indiana University Press, 1994, p. 39.

The French dramatist Ernest Legouvé has left an account of the emotional effect that the playing of Franz Liszt — another pioneer of Beethoven's music in France — could have on individuals. The occasion in question was a private soirée attended by a small, but highly select, audience of connoisseurs. Legouvé describes how Liszt took his place at the piano and, as he puts it,

> 'began the funereal and heart-rending *Adagio* of the Sonata in C-sharp minor [Op. 27, No. 2]'.

He himself was seated in an armchair and was disturbed by

'stifled sobs and moans'. He turned to look, only to see they came from non other than Hector Berlioz.

As recalled in: Alan Walker, *Franz Liszt. Volume 1, The virtuoso years: 1811-1847*, New York: Alfred A. Knopf, 1983, Vol. 1, p. 182.

Berlioz's emotional temperament was tested on a similar occasion following one of the first performances in France of Beethoven's Fifth Symphony. When a friend suggested to Berlioz the work merely 'showed talent', Berlioz had to be restrained from attacking him!

A further anecdote connects Franz Liszt and Hector Berlioz. Liszt is known to have conferred his own formidable energy on his interpretations of Beethoven. In the summer of 1836, Liszt gave a pioneering recital at the Salon Érard in Paris at which he performed Beethoven's challenging Piano Sonata Op. 106, *The Hammerklavier*. Hector Berlioz, in his capacity as a writer on music, recalled the event in the June issue of the *Revue et gazette musicale*. He writes: 'Never, perhaps, has this great artist excited the Parisian world to such a degree ...'.

Berlioz considered Liszt to be an exponent of 'the great modern school of piano-playing'. In support of his contention he enthused:

> 'I appeal to the judgement of all those who have heard him play the great *Hammerklavier* Sonata, that sublime poem which until now has been the riddle of the Sphinx for almost every pianist. Liszt, a new Oedipus, has solved it in a manner which would have made the composer, had he heard it in his grave, thrill with pride and joy.'

Berlioz continues in a similarly fulsome manner, paying tribute to Liszt being faithful to the score; although he is known, on occasions, to have added decorative flourishes and double octaves of his own devising. On the evening in question, Berlioz, who was following the performance from a copy of the score, could detect

> 'not a single alteration made to what was indicated in the text, not an inflexion or an idea weakened or changed its true meaning'.

Derived from: Adrian Williams, *Portrait of Liszt: By himself and his contemporaries*. 1990, pp. 79—80. The original review appeared in the *Revue et gazette musicale* 12 June 1836.

ARTHUR BLISS

The English composer Arthur Bliss writes of his early musical experiences whilst at preparatory school:

> 'I shall always be grateful to the self-effacing and dedicated music master there who introduced me to the Beethoven Sonatas ... My introduction to Beethoven through practising his *Andante con Variazioni*, Op. 26, and then through hearing in London his *Coriolan* Overture and Fifth Symphony fired me with a longing to find out all there was to know about his personality and life.'

In the spring of 1934, Bliss was invited to deliver a series of lectures at the Royal Institution. H. G. Wells was in the audience of one of these and later invited Bliss to compose the music to Alexander Korda's film-adaptation of his *Things to Come*. In discussing unity and form in music, Bliss made a passing, but significant, reference to Beethoven:

'[Unity] in diversity [is] the employment not of one idea that spreads, but of two or more antagonistic ideas that are gradually compelled to harmonize and form one complete whole. This implies drama and struggle, and is the formal idea lying behind the first movement of a Beethoven sonata, for instance. The first develops from a single thematic idea, the second is based on the interaction of several contrasted ones.'

Arthur Bliss, *As I remember*, London: Thames Publishing, 1989, pp. 18—19 and p.102.

ERNST BLOCH
In his essays on *The Philosophy of Music*, Ernst Bloch discusses the spirit in Beethoven's piano sonatas:

'Passion, pain, cheerfulness and liberation are and always will be the components of the sonata, as the authentic and encompassing Beethovenian form. The headings *Allegro, Adagio, Scherzo* and *Finale* generally correspond to these, although, on occasion to be sure, there is marked change in meaning. The first movement itself is frequently anything but an allegro, while the last occasionally incorporates rondo and even variation form. Normally the latter is diametrically opposed to strict, antithetical development. But when located in the final movement, it nonetheless constitutes the most significant part of the sonata besides the opening movement, precisely because it expands at will, loosely, more feely'.

*

Discussing modern-day interpretation of Beethoven, Bloch remarks:

> 'Young pianists often fail to give convincing accounts of the last Beethoven sonatas not because of technical difficulty or lack of intellectual understanding but because of insufficient emotional maturity. Their personal histories offer them no parallel to help them gauge the expressive potential of the music.'

Ernst Bloch, *Essays on the Philosophy of Music*, Cambridge: Cambridge University Press, 1985, p. 32 and p. 170.

ERIC BLOM

The musicologist, music critic and editor (notably of the 5th edition of Grove's *Dictionary of Music and Musicians,* 1954) gave the following estimation of Beethoven:

> 'Beethoven, as we as know, was an impossible man to live with; but though the intractable personality peeps out everywhere from the sonata, they not only proved endurable; they have endured. Their greatness has softened the composer's asperities and rudenesses and made them for us, over and above their purely musical wonders, into an intensely individual expression of the most irresistible fascination. Though we could not, any of us, have lived with Beethoven for a week, we still live with his sonatas, and the world, will go on doing so as it has such civilization of the mind to keep in spite of its failure to

attain to that universal brotherhood of mankind
that was Beethoven's delusion.'

Derived from the introductory text to, *Pianoforte Sonatas Op. 78, Op. 90 and Op. 111, The Beethoven Society*, Volume One (undated, c.1938). See also: Eric Blom, *Beethoven's Pianoforte Sonatas Discussed*, London: J. M. Dent, 1938.

ALFRED BRENDEL

Alfred Brendel is universally acknowledged for being among the greatest interpreters of Beethoven and has the distinction of being the first performer to record his complete solo works for piano. Writing of the piano sonatas he remarks:

'Beethoven's piano sonatas are unique in three respects. First, they represent the whole development of a genius, from his beginnings to the threshold of the late quartets. There are the *Diabelli* Variations and the last set of Bagatelles [to] round out the picture. Secondly, there is hardly a work among them that is not worth playing — in contrast to many sets of variations, for example, which tend to be uneven. I find it impossible to share Busoni's low opinion of Beethoven's early works. If we must divide Beethoven's works into three periods, in line with Liszt's pronouncement "l'adolescent, l'homme, le dieu", then the young Beethoven already stands there as a great composer. We must not take the term "adolescent" too literally, however, after all Beethoven was twenty-four when his Opus 1 was published. Thirdly, Beethoven does not repeat himself in his sonatas: each work, each movement is a new organism.'

From the same source as that just cited (see below), Brendel adds the following:

'Beethoven's autographs are often difficult to read, but it would be wrong to conclude from this that his notation, let alone his composition, was imprecise. The chaotic side of Beethoven's nature, so startlingly apparent from the scrawl of his handwriting, is brought to order in the finished compositions. The effort it cost him to achieve that order gives it its particular stability. However, Beethoven's untiring labour over details hardly ever interferes with his conception of the whole ... Beethoven was not primarily a stage composer, though I very much love his *Fidelio*; but he knew how to avoid repeating himself in his characters. That is also why playing his thirty-two piano sonatas is so satisfying, because taken as a whole they are all necessary, at least as contrasts to each other.'

Alfred Brendel, *Alfred Brendel on Music: Collected essays*. Chicago, Ilinois: A Cappella Books, 2001, p. 31 and p. 42.

In conversation with Brendel, the Swiss writer Martin Meyer invited him to place his gift for music alongside his other interests. Brendel replied:

'When I was very young, about sixteen, I went through a phase of playing a game with friends in which you had to pair composers with painters ...

We used to agree about the following pairings: Mozart-Watteau, Beethoven-Michelangelo. And then I read in an essay by a very earnest and famous colleague that Beethoven was like Michelangelo, only greater! If I needed something to put an end to such a game, that was it.'

When asked about the particular challenges posed by Beethoven's piano music, Brendel remarked:

'These are for me, as a performer, the most important points: to understand the concentration, then to convey the processional manner of the composition, the inevitability, the logic, in other words the erection of a building structure, block upon block, in order to achieve something especially stable. Finally, the quality of feeling, the genuineness, yes, the poetry of feeling, if such a phrase can be used today, without making people laugh.'

Alfred. Brendel, *The Veil of Order*. Alfred Brendel in conversation with Martin Meyer, London: Faber and Faber, 2002, p. 74 and p.106.

In conversation with the pianist and musicologist David Dubal, Alfred Brendel remarked:

'For me, Beethoven, a master of the Classical style, always shows the listener where the music goes, and always justifies why it goes there. He also gives the reasons for why it happens as it does. I do not mean that Beethoven is in any way predictable, but that it is his plan to explain

> himself throughout. In other words, Beethoven is in control.'

Alfred Brendel in conversation with David Dubal in: David Dubal, *The World of the Concert Pianist*, London: Victor Gollancz, 1985, p. 95.

Brendel concluded his remarks to Dubal saying:

> 'The marvellous thing about Beethoven's sonatas is that they are so different, each of them. Even sonatas of the same period can be so unlike each other. That's one of the reasons I love to play the cycle because there is virtually nothing that repeats itself. The scope of the imagination is so astounding that I would really call it mysterious. It's something one cannot explain by just looking at the person. Beethoven the man had his limitations and frailties, but as a composer he encompassed and mastered nearly everything that is human. And of course the last sonata is an essence of this humanity; it is a true conclusion of the series.'

Dubal, p. 111.

BENJAMIN BRITTEN

In 1963 the musicologist Murray Schafer interviewed Benjamin Britten and asked him about his sympathies towards Beethoven and Brahms. Britten responded:

> 'I'm not blind to them. Once I adored them. Between the ages of thirteen and fourteen, I knew every note of Beethoven and Brahms. I remem-

ber receiving the full score of *Fidelio* for my fourteenth birthday. It was a red letter day.'

Of his present day feelings toward Beethoven he added:

'I certainly don't dislike all Beethoven but sometimes I feel I have lost the point of what he's up to. I heard recently [1963] the Piano Sonata Op. 111. The sound of the variations was so grotesque I just couldn't see what they were about.'

Original source: Murray Schafer, *British Composer's Interview*, London, Faber and Faber, 1963, pp. 113–24. See also: Paul Kildea, editor, *Britten on Music*, Oxford: Oxford University Press, 2003, p. 228.

HANS VON BÜLOW

Although remembered today as one of the most famous conductors of the 19th century, and for his aphorism 'Bach is the Old Testament and Beethoven the New Testament of music', recollections from his early days remind us of his formidable powers as a virtuoso pianist. He pioneered the innovation of performing the complete series of Beethoven piano sonatas and was known for the challenging nature of some of his recitals — challenging both to himself and his audience. On one occasion von Bülow played the last five Beethoven piano sonatas in a single evening and on another occasion he opened his recital with a performance of the *Hammerklavier* Piano Sonata and concluded the evening with the *Diabelli* Variations.

As recalled in: Peter Yates, *Twentieth Century Music: Its evolution from the end of the harmonic era into the present era of sound*, London: Allen & Unwin Ltd., 1968.

The Czech composer and music critic Joseph Foerster has left recollections of Hamburg's musical scene in the late nineteenth century. In particular, he recalls the exacting demands von Bülow imposed upon himself. Foerster writes:

> 'His effervescent spirit could bear no easy-going manner approach, his pure artistry no half measures.'

He recalls the occasion when von Bülow was performing the F-sharp major Piano Sonata in Hamburg's Konviksaal. Although he was well into his performance he stopped because one string of the piano was out of tune, only resuming when the problem was rectified. In his role as orchestral conductor, von Bülow could be no less demanding of his audience. There was the occasion, for example, when, following a performance of Beethoven's Ninth symphony, he thanked the audience for their applause, apologised that Beethoven, who should receive it, could not attend but as a mark of respect proceeded to have the whole of the Finale repeated.

As recalled in: Kurt Blaukopf and Herta Blaukopf, *Mahler: His life, work and world*, London: Thames and Hudson, 1991, p. 92.

FERRUCCIO BUSONI

The Italian composer and pianist Ferruccio Busoni revealed his remarkable aptitude for piano at an early age, being elected to the Academia Filharmonica of Bologna at just fifteen — the youngest person to receive the honour since Mozart. In the summer of 1898, Busoni had occasion to write to his wife Gerda who had requested advice concerning practicing the piano. Although Busoni's response touches upon Beethoven but briefly, the following selection from his 'maxims', as he called them, has continuing relevance to would-be pianists:

> 'Practice the passage with the most difficult fingering; when you have mastered that, play it with the easiest.'

> 'If a passage offers some particular technical difficulty, go through all similar passages you can remember in other pieces; in this way you will bring system into the kind of playing in question.'

> 'Always join technical practice with the study of the interpretation; the difficulty, often, does not lie in the notes but in the dynamic shading.'

> 'Never be carried away by temperament, for that dissipates strength.'

> 'Study everything as if there were nothing more difficult; try to interpret studies for the young from the standpoint of the virtuoso. You will be astonished to find how difficult it is to play a Czerny, or Cramer, or even a Clementi.
> 'Never play carelessly, even when there is nobody listening, or the occasion seems unimportant.'

> 'If possible allow no day to pass without touching your piano.'

> 'Bach is the foundation of piano playing. Liszt the summit. The two make Beethoven possible.'

In the summer of 1907, Busoni had further occasion to write to Gerda — he was in Weimar on a concert tour. He told her of an amusing circumstance concerning his foremost pupil Egon Petrie:

> 'When Egon went over the German frontier, he had the Beethoven sonatas in his box, which were fished out at the customs. "What's that?" said the customs officer. That is music, the Beethoven sonatas [replied Petrie]. "Ah, *those* are the Beethoven sonatas." Said the customs officer and turned over the leaves. As regards the interpretation, he continued (as he gave back the volume), "There is nothing harder to play", and, he added, (for he took Egon for an Englishman) — "A foreigner cannot manage to do it; only a German can do it".'

Antony Beaumont, editor, *Ferruccio Busoni: Selected letters*, London: Faber and Faber, 1987, pp. 27—8 and p. 118.

ELLIOTT CARTER

In a BBC broadcast in the summer of 1972, the American composer Elliott Carter discussed the problem in musical appreciation of attaching words and meaning to sounds. He made a wry reference to Beethoven:

> 'Beethoven's answer to someone who asked questions about some music he had just played was to play it over again. This is, of course, the composer's true response about his own work.'

Else Stone and Kurt Stone, editors, *The Writings of Elliott Carter. An American composer looks at modern music*, Bloomington: Indiana University Press, 1977, p. 310.

JOHN V. COCKSHOT

In his analysis of the fugue in Beethoven's piano music, the musicologist John V. Cockshot concludes:

> 'We may be sure that Beethoven studied closely all the works of Bach which were available to him, but he remained true to his own genius by adapting fugal techniques to his special needs, and investing them with all the poetry of which he was capable. The fugues in Beethoven's piano music, particularly the late ones, are then the rich result of the fertilization of the best elements of the Viennese school with those of Bach. They are irreplaceable in those works of Beethoven which rank among his greatest, and always show him to be completely the master in every degree of technique and emotion.'

John V. Cockshot, *The Fugue in Beethoven's Piano Music*, London: Routledge & Kegan Paul, 1959, p. 184.

MARTIN COOPER

In the context of the study of Beethoven's works for piano, the English musicologist and pianist Martin Cooper cites Anton Schindler (see below):

> 'The study of Beethoven's music should not be

begun seriously until the student has reached an advanced state of general as well as purely musical culture, without which it will have an exhausting effect on those who have little sensibility to musical poetry. The music sprang in the first place from a profound personality and it is only fully intelligible and useful to profound personalities.'

Cooper adds his own views to Schindler's exhortations:

'Although the works of Beethoven's early and middle years are technically within the grasp of many young artists and have become so much part of the language of music that they are "understood" by all musically educated people, many of them still demand a quality of musical perception and depth of emotional experience that no child can posses (and many of the technically most brilliant and most sophisticated young artists are still emotionally children). The works of Beethoven's last years, including all five of the last piano sonatas, should be regarded, like great operatic roles, as something that no physical, or even intellectual gifts, however exceptional, justify a young artist in attempting.'

Martin Cooper, *Beethoven: The last decade, 1817-1827*, London: Oxford University Press, 1970, p. 187.

CARL CZERNY

Carl Czerny received piano lessons from Beethoven at the age of ten. By his own account, by he could then play all the works of Mozart with the exception of a few that were beyond the reach of his young fingers. He recalls with 'what joy and terror I greeted the day on which I was to meet the admired master'.

He found the composer's room presented a most disorderly appearance; papers and articles of clothing were scattered about everywhere. The walls were bare and hardly a chair was to be seen 'save the wobbly one at the Walter fortepiano'.

Czerny is referring here to the fortepiano Beethoven owned at this time made by the celebrated Viennese maker Anton Walter. Czerny discerned Beethoven wearing a morning coat of some long grey material and trousers to match – he thought he looked like Robinson Crusoe! He also noticed the composer had cotton wool protruding from his ears 'steeped in a yellowish liquid' – doubtless indicative of one of Beethoven's many attempts to find relief for his failing hearing.

At Beethoven's request to play, Czerny responded with a rendering of Mozart's great C major Piano Concerto, K. 503. Beethoven, after some initial hesitation, supplied the orchestral melody with his left hand. Czerny continues:

> 'The satisfaction he expressed gave me the courage to play his *Sonata Pathétique* which had just appeared.'

At the conclusion of the piece, Beethoven turned to Czerny's father and said: 'The boy has talent. I will teach him myself and accept him as my pupil.'

The reminiscences of Carl Czerny are recalled in: Oscar George Theodore Sonneck, *Beethoven: Impressions of contemporaries.* London: Oxford University Press, 1927, pp. 25–7.

Czerny further relates that Beethoven's first lessons concentrated on practice of all the scales and the adoption of a good hand position, the latter being, as Czerny remarks: 'Something at the time still unknown to most players.'

His audition with Beethoven must have been doubly challenging since a number of distinguished musicians were also present, including Mozart's pupil Franz Süssmayr.

It is from Czerny we learn:

> 'Since his youth, Beethoven had been accepted and honoured by the most illustrious circles, and he was always at home and quite at ease in their midst; he made his superiority felt by one and all, especially as a young man.'

With the onset of the composer's deafness, he adds:

> 'Until about 1816 he could still hear himself playing, by using a mechanical aid, [Czerny is referring here to the ear trumpets designed for him by Maelzel] but even that became increasingly difficult in time, and he had to depend on his inner ear, his imagination and experience.'

Czerny studied many of Beethoven's piano sonatas under the direct supervision of the composer, who, with the onset of deafness, entrusted him with the first performance of a number of his works for piano including the Piano Concerto in E-flat major, the *Emperor*, and the *Hammerklavier* Piano Sonata. In later years, Czerny published notes on the *proper performance* of Beethoven's works for piano which include the following challenging points of guidance:

'There are ... important conditions which are indispensably necessary, and upon which everything else depends, namely:

'The right time...

'The accurate observance of all the marks of expression which Beethoven, particularly in his later works, has very carefully indicated...

'The thorough mastery of all difficulties and the cultivation of a good execution in all respects, which must have been previously acquired by the study of other excellent composers...

'With the application of these three necessary conditions, we cannot fail in seizing the spirit of Beethoven's works...

'The higher intellectual conception can only be acquired, even with innate talent, by an intimate acquaintance with all Beethoven's compositions, by means of an experienced teacher, and by all that we have endeavoured to point out, to the best of our ability.'

Carl Czerny, *On the Proper Performance of all Beethoven's Works for the Piano,* in: Paul Badura-Skoda, editor and co-translator, Universal Edition: A. G. Wien, 1970, p. 108.

Other remarks attributed to Czerny include the following.

ON THE BEAUTY OF TONE

'Whoever possesses the art of always producing from the pianoforte a beautiful, harmonious and smooth tone; who never carries the forte or fortissimo to a disagreeable and excessive harshness; and further who combines the highest degree of volubility with perfect distinctness and clearness, will execute even the most startling assemblage of notes, so that they shall appear beautiful, even to persons unacquainted with music; and give them unfeigned delight.'

On the style of execution most suitable to different composers and their works:

MOZART'S SCHOOL

'A distinct and considerably brilliant manner of playing, calculated rather on the staccato than on the legato touch; and intelligent and animated execution, the pedal seldom used, and never obbligato.'

BEETHOVEN'S STYLE

'Characteristic and impassioned energy, alternating with all the charms of smooth and connected cantabile, is in its place here. The means of expression is often carried to excess, particularly in regard to humorous and fanciful levity. The piquant, brilliant, and showy manner is but seldom applicable here: but for this reason, we must the more frequently attend to the total effect, partly by means of a full, harmonious legato, and partly by a happy use of the pedals &c. Great volubility of finger without brilliant pretentions, and in the *adagio*, enthusiastic expression and singing melody, replete with sentiment and pathos, are the great requisites in the player.'

Czerny concludes:

> 'The player who desires to arrive at anything like perfection, must dedicate a considerable space of time exclusively to the compositions of each master who has founded a school; till he has not only accustomed his mind to the peculiar style of each, but also, till he is enabled to remain faithful to it, in the mechanical performance of their works.'

Carl Czerny: *Technique Personified*, in: Reginald Gerig, *Famous Pianists & their Technique*, Washington: R. B. Luce, 1974, pp. 103–20.

CARL DAHLHAUS

The German musicologist Carl Dahlhaus outlined his views on the music of Beethoven in his *Ludwig van Beethoven: Approaches to his music*. Translated by Mary Whittall, Oxford: Clarendon Press; New York: Oxford University Press, 1991. In one of his generalizations he remarks:

> 'Beethoven overwhelmed the limits of Classical form in his sonata movements by blurring the demarcations between sections and theme-groups and in creating such gigantic structures as the first movements of the *Hammerklavier* Sonata and the Ninth Symphony.'

Carl Dahlhaus, *Nineteenth-Century Music*, translated by J. Bradford Robinson, Berkeley; London: University of California Press, 1989, p. 29.

*

CLAUDE DEBUSSY

The French composer's antipathy towards Beethoven frequently found expression in several of his utterances. In 1909, Debussy was a somewhat reluctant member of the jury for the piano examinations at the Paris Conservatoire. In a letter to Albert Carré, Director of the *Opéra Comique*, he gave vent to his pejorative views about his fellow-jury members and the piano music of Beethoven:

> 'I've been dedicating myself to the betterment of the pianistic race in France ... The jury included some odd musicians who'd have been more at home, I fancy, judging livestock. And I came to the unshakable conclusion on two points: that Beethoven wrote really badly for the piano and that there exists a mysterious correlation between people's ugliness and the music they choose.'

François Lesure and Roger Nichols, editors, *Debussy, Letters*, London: Faber and Faber, 1987.

ANTONÍN DVORÁK

Writing about her father, Otakar Dvorák relates: 'Some critics have not taken my father seriously as a composer because he did not have much of an education ... But father's self-education and, of course, his talent gave him more than any music conservatory could have. He said to me, "How much time I spent learning the rich forms of Beethoven's sonatas!" ' Recalling a later occasion she adds:

> 'Father adored Mozart and Beethoven. A very small bust of Mozart's head stood on Father's desk, and next to that a small picture of the

gloomy face of Beethoven. Once after a concert
Father received a wreath inscribed with the words,
"To the greatest genius ever." Father took this
wreath home and draped the ribbon over the
picture of Beethoven.'

Otakar Dvorák, *Antonín Dvorák, My father*, Spillville, Iowa:
Czech Historical Research Center, 1993, p. 91 and p. 109.

GEORGE DYSON

The English musician and composer Sir George Dyson was
invited to contribute to Beethoven's *Death Centenary* (1927)
in a special edition of *The Musical Times*. The following is
an extract from his essay concerning questions of expression
and interpretation — couched in suitably laudatory terms:

'The outstanding pianist will always demand
problems of interpretation on which to feed the
zeal of his evangel. For him Beethoven is food
indeed. And there has been no player of high
rank who has not counted it a triumph to present
to the world, at whatever expense of labour and
thought, the truth of a message so exacting. In the
pursuit of expression Beethoven was merciless.
Pianoforte, quartet, orchestra and chorus, all alike
he stretched to the utmost. He forgets that there
are limits to the powers of an instrument, limits
to the capacity of a human interpreter. Above all,
he forgets himself. He would crouch under the
desk to suggest a *pianissimo*. He would gesticulate
wildly and ludicrously to emphasize a *fortissimo*.
He would caress the piano into quiet ecstasies
which his friends never forgot. He would thrash

it into turmoil that made them almost afraid. Moods so intense are not for every man, though there can be no supreme artists without them. When the heat of his passion demands the impossible, it is because his vision is of things beyond man's power to describe. In pursuit of that transcendence Beethoven spent himself. And if his fire sometimes scorches us it consumed his own ardent soul no less.'

George Dyson, in: *Music & Letters, Beethoven:* Special Number, London: 1927, p. 21.

ALFRED EINSTEIN

The German-American musicologist Alfred Einstein (considered by some authorities to be distantly related to the celebrated mathematician) is best known for his revision of the Köchel Catalogue of Mozart. His musical writings, however, are wide ranging and include the following references to Beethoven's piano sonatas:

'There are no "lengths" — heavenly or otherwise — in Beethoven, because he took over forms; instead, he created them anew. Beethoven had his characteristic formulae, but they were never empty husks, and he never repeated himself. The Romantics were of the opinion that in his last works — in the piano sonatas from Op. 101 to Op. 111, and especially in the last quartets — he had "burst form asunder"; and from this illustrious model they developed the idea that it was permissible or justifiable that they themselves should deal as freely as possible with form. As a matter of fact, there is not — even in these last works of Beethoven's — a single movement, a single measure, that does not rest on the strictest, immanent musical logic, and that even in the most minute detail would call for extra-musical justification.'

In his opening remarks, Einstein is making reference to Robert Schumann's evaluation of the piano sonatas of Franz Schubert to which he, Schumann, attributed "heavenly lengths".

Alfred Einstein, *Music in the Romantic era*, London: J.M. Dent Ltd., 1947, p. 66.

In the spring of 1933 Einstein attended a series of recitals given by Artur Schnabel. The following is taken from his review of these:

'Artur Schnabel's undertaking to play all the Beethoven sonatas, in seven concerts, was as much an event for Berlin as it was for London. Schnabel has once again demonstrated that he is a great artist. His recordings of Beethoven are full of rare intelligence, which never impair the tonal beauty. He gives every sonata its own peculiar character but one which is always that of Beethoven.'

Catherine Dower, *Alfred Einstein on Music: Selected music criticisms,* New York: Greenwood Press, 1991, p. 135.

ERNST VON ELTERLEIN

In 1856 the musicologist and musician Ernst von Elterlein published an influential book on the subject of Beethoven's piano sonatas. It achieved considerable popularity throughout Germany and went through several editions and is still held in high regard with facsimile editions being published. An English edition first appeared in 1875 in a translation by E. Pauer. Introducing his text, Pauer prepares the reader with the following remarks:

> 'The transcendent beauty and the exceeding importance of Beethoven's pianoforte sonatas are facts now universally recognised. It is a healthy sign of musical progress, and an undeniable proof of the spread of an improved taste and of a genuine appreciation of the excellent in musical art, that various nations now emulate each other's efforts in issuing correct and excellent editions of these great works. Herr von Elterlein's design is not so much to describe the beauties of Beethoven's sonatas, as to direct the performer's attention to these beauties, and to point out the leading characteristic features of each separate piece. It was reserved for Beethoven to give expression, in his sonatas, to the highest and loftiest feelings of the human heart. In these unapproachable masterpieces, he is not only pathetic, but also sincere, humorous, tender, graceful, simple — in short, he expresses in them every varying shade of feeling that can agitate the human heart.'

In the first edition von Elterlein himself states:

> 'Beethoven was not all at once what he became in his prime. The gradual growth and ripening of his mind — surely one of the most interesting psychological periods in the course of a great

artist's evolution — is more clearly illustrated in his sonatas than in his other works. Nowhere else are those fine gradual changes, that progress towards an ever increasing independence, so noticeable and so traceable ... In Beethoven, imagination, feeling, intellect, and character are developed with equal potency and import, and in perfect harmony with each other. It is to these fundamentals that the finest works seem to me to be their inevitable outcome.'

Of the piano sonatas in particular, von Elterlein remarks:

'The sonata is the greatest and most original production in the province of pianoforte music — its highest exercise and its loftiest aim. Beauty, the ideal of all artistic efforts, may be expressed in the simplest music, but its complete realization can only be attained in the highest forms.'

The German-American musicologist Alfred Einstein (considered by some authorities to be distantly related to the celebrated mathematician) is best known for his revision of the Köchel Catalogue of Mozart. His musical writings, however, are wide ranging and include the following references to Beethoven's piano sonatas:

'[The] object of the sonata is to display a rich, expressive, and subjective state of feeling, whether this flows forth in a rich full stream of emotional images, or whether, in the form of a great tone-picture, one of the different phases of the prevailing sentiment of the emotional life is depicted.'

*

Concluding a review of the editions of Beethoven's piano sonatas, available to von Elterlein at the time of the publication of the first edition of his book, he affirms:

> 'Thus will Beethoven's music extend into an ever-widening circle, the number of Beethoven's friends will increase from year to year, and the temple of true musical beauty will be more widely opened and become a greater blessing to mankind.'

Ernst von Elterlein, *Beethoven's Pianoforte Sonatas: Explained for the lovers of the musical art*, London: W. Reeves, 1898, pp. 1–3, pp. 31–3 and p. 141.

DOROTHEA VON ERTMANN

Dorothea von Ertmann was one of the most gifted pianists of her day and one of the foremost interpreters of Beethoven's piano sonatas. She received lessons from the composer, earning from him the affectionate soubriquet *Dorothea Cecilia* – a thinly disguised reference to *Sancta Caecilia*, the patroness of musicians. When her only child died at a young age, Beethoven sought to console her by improvising at the piano for more than an hour.

In the winter of 1808 the composer Johann Reinhardt, at one time in the service of Frederick the Great, heard her play. His account of Ertmann's performance sheds light on how Beethoven's piano sonatas were being assimilated into the repertoire of gifted performers of the day and into the society of the nobility more generally. Reinhardt recalls:

> '[As] she performed a great Beethoven Sonata [unspecified] I was surprised as almost never

before. I have never seen such power and innermost tenderness combined even in the greatest virtuosi; from the tip of each finger her soul poured forth, and from her hands, both equally skillful and sure, what power and authority were brought to bear over the whole instrument.'

As recalled in: Elliot Forbes, editor, *Thayer's Life of Beethoven*, Princeton, New Jersey: Princeton University Press, 1967, p. 412.

In July 1831, Felix **Mendelssohn heard** Dorothea play when he visited her in Milan during his tour of Italy. Writing to his sister Fanny he gave the following account of her playing and its influence upon him:

'She plays Beethoven's works [the piano sonatas] admirably, though it is so long since she studied them she sometimes rather exaggerates the expression, dwelling too long on one passage, and hurrying the next; but there are many parts she plays splendidly, and I think I have learned something from her.'

Bartholdy Mendelssohn, *Letters from Italy and Switzerland*, London: Longman, Green, Longman, and Roberts, 1862, p. 203.

Beethoven's secretary and early biographer Anton Schindler considered Ertmann's interpretation of Beethoven's piano music to be without equal, revealing a natural grasp 'of even the most hidden subtleties'.

He adds:

'She knew how to give each phrase the motion of its particular spirit, how to move artistically from

> one phrase to the next, so that the whole seemed
> a motivated unity.'

In Schindler's estimation: 'She was a conservatoire all by herself.'

It appears her playing was distinguished by its intimacy and expressiveness rather than by showy physicality. It is known she declined to perform any work that did not suit her style, following her self-imposed maxim: 'Not everything is appropriate for everyone.'

Dorothea was apparently a pianist who made up for her lack of physical strength by the sensitivity of her playing. According to Schindler's testimony, it was as a consequence of her championing of Beethoven's piano sonatas, in later years, that did much to save them from neglect and helped them to maintain their place in the repertoire. As several commentators have concluded, given the poetic nature of Ertmann's style of performance – and the personal regard Beethoven had for her playing – it is not surprising he should dedicate his A major Piano Sonata (Op. 101) to her, imbued as it is with so many of the pianistic qualities to which Dorothea von Ertmann was so intuitively inclined.

Anton Felix Schindler, *Beethoven as I Knew Him*, edited by Donald W. MacArdle and translated by Constance S. Jolly from the German edition of 1860, London: Faber and Faber, 1966, pp. 210–11.

BRIAN FERNEYHOUGH

The English composer Brian Ferneyhough was interviewed in 1990 by the musicologist James Boros. They discussed the question of contemporary performance-practice, prompting the following response from Ferneyhough:

> 'In previous ages it was never performances which survived, but only scores, notated music. If all the information necessary to a correct interpretation is not in a score, it is practically impossible to reconstruct original intentions with a degree of certainty. Only tradition can provide some sort of tenuous continuity in this respect. If you play a Beethoven sonata, you're not interpreting the notes on the page, you're interpreting many generations of interpretation, an entire corpus of slowly evolving conventions.'

James Boros and Richard Toop, editors, *Brian Ferneyhough: Collected writings*, Amsterdam: Harwood Academic, 1995, pp. 375–6.

EDWIN FISCHER

Amongst his many accomplishments, the Swiss classical pianist and conductor Edwin Fischer was an acknowledged interpreter of Beethoven's piano music. He outlined his views in his *Ludwig van Beethovens Klaviersonaten: Ein Begleiter für Studierende und Liebhaber*, 1954 (*Beethoven's Piano Sonatas: A Guide for Students and Amateurs*, 1959). In his introductory remarks he observes:

> 'Ludwig van Beethoven's work has the quality of true greatness. What worlds he traversed from the simple beginnings to the sublimation that he achieved at the close of his life's struggle! ... If, in his beginnings, sheer delight in the resources of the piano predominates, later on the interest in structure and symphonic form becomes more

and more evident. With Opp. 27 and 31 a more
romantic, "pianistic", trend emerges once more,
bringing with it a freer treatment of form. These
sonatas in fantasia style also introduce the greatest
advancers in the harmonic sphere. Thereafter
Beethoven uses all manner of forms, orchestral,
variations, even fugue, to aid him in the portrayal
of his visions: we have now those magnificent
contests between Beethoven's personality and the
world, those demonstrations of his creative will.
In the childlike themes which he uses in Opp.
109, 110 and 111 he now achieves the ideal of
symbolizing the highest in terms of the greatest
simplicity. What was, at the outset, the expression
of a personal faith, is transferred into an expression of eternal, universal truth.'

Reflecting on the varying styles of interpretation of these works, as found in the printed editions of the sonatas or as he had experienced them in the concert hall, Fischer adds:

'It goes without saying that an artist's interpretation of a particular work is just as dependent on the environment from which he comes as on the schools [of piano studies] where he acquired his skill and knowledge ... There is a piano "method" by Carl Czerny which contains many references to Beethoven's own character and performances.'

Fischer is referring here to Czerny's Op. 500, *Complete Theoretical and Practical Pianoforte School*, which includes his commentary: *On the Proper Performance of all Beethoven's Works for the Piano.*

*

Fischer continues:

> 'The Liszt tradition was probably based very largely on this. [Liszt was a pupil of Czerny.] His edition was a rather personal one, however, and is no longer entirely acceptable. He was followed by Eugène d'Albert and Hans von Bülow, masters whom I heard myself. Von Bülow, a man of great wit, and a strong personality, had a wide influence at a time when the general musical public was still in need of enlightenment. Quite aware of this state of affairs, he dispensed instruction in his recitals by boldly underlining his convictions. He had a habit of performing little-known works twice in succession, notably the great Sonata Op. 106. His edition of the *Diabelli Variations* is invaluable. Eugène d'Albert was more a man of the concert-platform. His healthy and vigorous style of playing was an example to us all.'

Fischer concludes:

> 'The most helpful counsel one can give is this: "Love him and his work, and you will inevitably become his servant and interpreter and yet remain yourself. Your energy, your warmth and your love will kindle his energy, his spirit and his love in the hearts of men and make them shine therein".'

Edwin Fischer, *Beethoven's Pianoforte Sonatas: A guide for students & amateurs*, London: Faber and Faber, 1959, pp.15–18 and pp. 67–8.

*

In 1921 Fischer was invited to give an address on the subject of musical interpretation. Beethoven featured substantially in his remarks:

> 'What glorious things he [Beethoven] has entrusted to the piano, whole symphonies, string quartets, organ pieces, arias, choral movements, recitative, string fugues, and, in addition, what is peculiarly pianistic — all this he has written for the piano. And what delight and happiness he offered the player! Here there remains something for the interpreter to do, he must puzzle out, must colour, be an actor, exchange the orchestra for the organ, be a pianist, singer, string player — all in one! Is it to be wondered at that the great pianists have grown up through contact with this music?'

Concerning musical interpretation, Fischer remarks

> '*feel* Beethoven; let organ, violin, wind instruments, drum, singer sound again on the piano. Bring the whole world out of the shadowy kingdom of notation into the living light again; for all I care play the *Moonlight Sonata* as a lament for the dead, orchestrate the funeral march from Opus 26 in the most modern fashion. Conjure up today from the *Waldstein Sonata* such an idyll of nature, that tomorrow the world is up in arms against you and then, the day after, play it in formal perfection, as pure music, if your nature is such that you can delight in formal purity. Everything is there, you will gain wings that shall

carry you and others into the true realm of imagination, and show you where Beethoven's spirit sojourned ... The best way of serving Beethoven today, is, through an intensive study of his works, to attempt to draw nearer his ideal, divine mode of thought, his lofty spirit, and afterwards, in interpretation, by faithful reproduction to make a breath of this spirit alive.'

Edwin Fischer, *Reflections on Music*, London: Williams and Norgate, 1951, p. 32.

LEOPOLD GODOWSKY

In his lifetime the Polish pianist Leopold Godowsky was considered to be one of the most highly regarded of pianists; although almost self-taught, he made his first concert appearance at the age of fourteen. When just eleven years old he auditioned to be admitted to Berlin's Königliche Hochscule für Musik. Of this experience Godowsky recalled later in life how self-conscious he felt wearing short trousers before the board of judges — each 'poker-faced ... never betraying any emotion, for or against the pupil's playing'. It almost beggars belief that, at such a tender age, he performed the Piano Sonata Op. 81a.

After his performance, the young prodigy was kept at the piano for much longer than the other candidates who had preceded him in the examination, conveying the impression his playing had not pleased the judges. On the contrary, following their deliberations they asked the young Godowsky whether he could not merely play but could also transpose Mendelssohn's technically challenging Rondo Capriccioso, Op. 14 into another key — for which he was quite unprepared. He remarks:

> 'I played the transcription with astonishing accuracy for which I had no training in the art of transposition.'

Godowsky concludes his youthful recollections:

> 'When I was leaving the hall one of the gloomy judges approached me and handed his calling card which told me I was to have admittance to the artists' room for ... that night, and thereafter I found myself the door open to me.'

The 'gloomy judge' in question was the celebrated violinist Joseph Joachim.

As recounted by Jeremy Nicholas, *Godowsky: The pianists' pianist; A biography of Leopold Godowsky.* 1989, pp. 12–3.

STEWART GORDON

In his study of the history of writing for the piano, the American musician, teacher, writer, editor and composer Stewart Gordon comments:

> 'Although virtuoso elements, dramatic gesture, and even calculated roughness in which Beethoven has sometimes revelled are still present in the final sonatas, these are all combined with a fountainhead of spiritual energy from deep within the composer. The perception of this development in the composer's style has built a firm, well-founded belief among musicians and listeners that "late Beethoven" is music of

> great depth and spirituality, representing in music
> the eternal enigmas of life itself.'

Stewart Gordon, *A History of Keyboard Literature: Music for the piano and its forerunners*, Schirmer Books: New York; London: Prentice Hall International, 1996, p. 180.

PERCY GRAINGER

The Australian pianist and composer Percy Grainger gave his first public recital in Melbourne at the age of twelve — including works by Beethoven. Later in London, in the 1920s, *The Times* critic recorded that Grainger's playing "revealed rare intelligence and a good deal of artistic insight". At this time (1915) Grainger wrote an article in the magazine *Étude*, in which he expressed his delight in what he called "new forms of pianism", as he considered to be found in the piano writing of Debussy and Ravel — amongst others. He expressed reservations though about the writing for piano of certain masters of the past:

> 'The great composers, such as Bach and
> Beethoven, thought of the piano as a medium for
> all-round expression, but perhaps they did not so
> often feel inspired by its specifically pianistic
> attributes as do several of the moderns. Many of
> Beethoven's sonatas could be orchestrated and a
> symphonic effect produced.'

Malcolm Gillies and Bruce Clunies Ross, editors, *Grainger on Music*, Oxford; New York: Oxford University Press, 1999, p. 66.

*

SIR CHARLES HALLÉ

Charles Hallé was of German extraction and in his early years was renowned as a child prodigy – at the age of four, for example, he performed a sonatina in public. In his student days, in Paris, he associated with Frédéric Chopin and Franz Liszt. He moved to England in 1848, changing his name from Karl Halle to Charles Hallé, and became a favourite of the musical salons and a pioneer in the promotion of Beethoven's piano sonatas. Hallé was the first pianist in England to perform the complete series of the composer's piano sonatas, initially in recitals held at his own house and later in the St. James Concert Hall, Piccadilly. It has been said that it was due in great measure to Hallé's recitals 'that a knowledge of Beethoven's pianoforte sonatas became general in English society'.

Hallé recalls his initial experience of London recitals in 1848 when he made his début. He tells us: 'I may consider my first public appearance in England ... was favourably received and criticised.'

As a consequence, Hallé was invited to play for *The Musical Union*, then the most important concert institution for chamber music in London. This was originated in 1845 by the English violinist John Ella and existed until 1880, helping to shape and inform the wider public appreciation of music, alongside its sister concert series known as the *Popular Concerts*. When Hallé stated to Ella that he wished to play 'one of Beethoven's pianoforte sonatas' Ella exclaimed, 'Impossible!' and endeavoured to demonstrate to Hallé:

> 'They were not works to be played in public; that, as far as he knew, no solo sonata had ever before been included in any concert programme, and that he could not venture to offer one to his subscribers.'

*

Hallé further recalls how he had to battle for several days before Ella consented and who 'was much surprised to find that the sonata I had chosen [was] Op. 31, No. 3 in E-flat major'.

Ella's fears proved to be unfounded, as Hallé recounts: His performance 'pleased so much that several ladies who heard it arranged parties in order to hear it once more'.

Subsequently, Ella made no difficulty about Hallé performing other Beethoven sonatas, but he still cautioned the young pianist

> 'to be careful in their selection, and to choose those that could more easily be appreciated'.

Hallé duly acquiesced:

> 'I advanced therefore very cautiously, the second sonata I played being the one in D, Op. 28, commonly known as the *Pastorale*.'

Looking back on these years, in 1896 when he wrote his recollections, he records:

> '*Then* the question was: Can this or that [Beethoven] sonata be understood by the audience? Nowadays the difficulty lies in finding one not too hackneyed.'

Charles E. Hallé, 1896, pp. 103–4. Hallé's account is also recalled by Charles Rigby, see: *Sir Charles Hallé: A portrait today.* 1952, p. 66 and Michael Kennedy, *Hallé Tradition: A century of music.* 1960, p. 18.

It so chanced that Louis Spohr was in London in 1855

and heard Hallé perform the D major Piano Sonata Op. 10. After the concert, Spohr made some flattering remarks about Hallé's performance and proclaimed the D major to be 'a fine sonata', adding, 'not antiquated'.

The latter remark left Hallé somewhat perplexed. Was Spohr perhaps trying to say that he regarded the Piano Sonata Op. 10, No. 3 as modern sounding?

At about this same period George Bernard Shaw, in his capacity as a London music critic, also heard Hallé perform Beethoven's Sonata Op. 10, No. 3 at a recital in the City. He considered Hallé's artistry as being self-effacing, remarking — with characteristic wit:

> 'Sir Charles is not a sensational player ... The secret is that he gives you as little as possible of Hallé and as much as possible of Beethoven.'

Michael Kennedy, 1960, p. 72. Kennedy also tells the same anecdote in *The Autobiography of Charles Hallé*, 1972, p. 10. Shaw's own text, together with numerous of his other concert reviews, is published in: Bernard Shaw, *London Music, 1888-89*, 1937, pp. 41-2.

In 1853 Hallé moved to Manchester to direct what were known as the *Manchester's Gentleman's Concerts*. In due course Hallé enhanced their standing in the form of the Hallé Orchestra concert series, performed under his baton, and continuing to this day. During the concert season of 1870–1, by which time Hallé was better known to the public as a conductor, in fulfilment of a personal resolution, he gave a performance of the C-sharp minor Piano Sonata on the anniversary of Beethoven's death — which fell on 17 December 1870. In the event, the concert had to be given on 15 December and included so many other works of Beethoven's that it did not finish until 11.00 p.m.

Hallé regularly took the family for their summer holiday on the Isle of Wight, where they had a cottage at Cowes. His son recalls, affectionately, the delight of sitting in the garden on summer nights

> 'hearing the *Moonlight* and other divine sonatas [of Beethoven] played as only my father could play them'.

Michael Kennedy, 1960. The information cited is derived from a general reading of this source. The above quotation is taken from p. 81.

E. T. A. HOFFMAN

Ernst Theodor Amadeus Hoffmann was among the first of Beethoven's contemporaries to write reviews of Beethoven's compositions. His insights cast light on how Beethoven's music was received by the music-discerning public during Beethoven's lifetime. The following is an extract from an essay that originally appeared in 1813. In considering what Hoffman has to say, in his second paragraph, it should be borne in mind that in 1813 Beethoven's most technically challenging piano sonatas, such as the *Hammerklavier Sonata*, had yet to be composed:

> 'The seriousness, in all of Beethoven's works for instruments and for the piano, is in itself enough to forbid all those breakneck passages up and down for the two hands which fill our piano music in the latest style, all the queer leaps, the farcical capriccios, the notes towering high above the staff on their five-six line scaffold [ledger lines] ... On the other side of mere digital dexterity,

> Beethoven's compositions for the piano really present no special difficulty, for every player must be presumed to have in his fingers the few runs, triplet figures, and whatever else is called for; nevertheless, their performance is on the whole quite difficult. Many a so-called virtuoso condemns this music, objecting that it is "very difficult" and into the bargain "very ungrateful" ... Now, as regards difficulty, the correct and fitting performance of a work of Beethoven's asks nothing more than that one should understand him, that one should enter deeply into his being, that — conscious of ones own consecration — one should boldly dare to step into the circle of the magical phenomena that his powerful spell has evoked.'

E. T. A. Hoffman in: *Words on Music: From Addison to Barzun,* Jack Sullivan, editor, Athens: Ohio University Press, 1990, pp. 12–22.

VINCENT D'INDY

The French composer Vincent d'Indy taught for many years at the Paris Conservatoire where his instruction made reference to the works of Beethoven — he published a study of the composer in 1911. One of his pupils recalls:

> 'His teaching of sonata form stressed the tripartite division of exposition, development, and recapitulation; the exposition in its turn was divided into two main contrasting ideas, masculine and feminine in character, exemplified by the subjects of the first movement of Beethoven's *Hammerklavier Sonata,* Op. 106, forceful and lyrical respectively.'

In his analysis of this sonata, d'Indy considered Beethoven's development sections to be of 'such prodigious richness and an almost infinite variety as to defy rigorous classification'.

Enlarging on these observations, he adds:

> 'Each development bears the trace of a ripely pondered plan of construction: to each work corresponds a special plan which one can easily analyse: one discerns three periods of tonal transition and *immobility* alternating regularly; stages judiciously determined in keys related one to each other; modulations oriented towards the light or the shade.'

Andrew Thomson. *Vincent d'Indy and his World*, Oxford: Clarendon Press, 1996, pp. 130–1.

Remarking on the fate of the piano sonata following Beethoven's death d'Indy writes:

> 'Having cleared and lit up the way by these colossal beacons, Beethoven died; and, strange to say, at the moment not a single individual in the three artistic nations appeared to have observed these lights. Italy, the pride of music in the sixteenth century, was then in a condition of meretricious degeneracy, from which even now [early twentieth century] she has by no means rallied. France, caught in the toils of the Judaic school of opera, was producing nothing in the sphere of symphonic music ... As to Berlioz,

> passionate admirer of Beethoven as he shows himself in his writings — did he really understand him? ... At any rate, he remained as remote from him as possible in art; and it would be difficult to find more completely at the opposite poles of creative thought than the creator of the *Symphonie Fantastique* of the *La Damnation de Faust* and the mind that planned the *Missa Solemnis* and the Twelfth Quartet [Op. 127] ... As to Germany, she had in no way profited by Beethoven's indications; not a single composer attempted to take over this heritage, bequeathed, like the legendary sword of the Northern sages, to the worthiest.'

Vincent D' Indy, *César Franck*, New York: Dover Publications, 1965 (reprint), pp. 86–7.

WILLIAM KINDERMAN

American pianist and music scholar William Kinderman considers the musical and artistic legacy implicit in Beethoven's piano sonatas:

> 'The piano works of Beethoven comprise a vast musical legacy from all periods of his career and include a number of path-breaking compositions that anticipated his most outstanding achievements in other genres ... Beethoven's sonatas not only demonstrated his mastery of the Viennese classical style but also succeeded in considerable measure in defining the style itself. The influence of these works has been incalculable and has left an imprint not only on subsequent compositions

and performance traditions but also on the development of serious musical criticism and analysis, shaping the very ways in which we think about musical art.'

William Kinderman in: Larry R. Todd, editor, *Nineteenth-Century Piano Music*, New York; London: Routledge, 2004, pp. 55–6.

H. C. ROBBINS LANDON

The indefatigable musicologist H. C. Robbins Landon remarks:

> 'Beethoven's music ... owes much to his love of the piano as to his love of the string quartet; this is not just because the confidant of his study gave him all shades of *piano* and *forte*, all gradings of *crescendo* and *diminuendo*, a *staccato* as sharp as a harpsichord's and a *cantabile* smoother than a clavichord's, but because he could imagine himself controlling an orchestra or even a chorus with orchestra.'

H. C. Robbins Landon, editor, *The Mozart Companion*, London: Faber, 1956, pp. 32–3. For numerous other references to Beethoven and his works, see: H. C. Robbins Landon, *Beethoven: A documentary study*, London: Thames and Hudson, 1970.

THEODOR LESCHETIZKY

The eminent Polish pianist Theodor Leschetizky was a pupil of Carl Czerny who in turn had been a pupil of Beethoven.

Leschetizky recalls how proud Czerny was to have been his pupil and described his time in Beethoven's company so vividly that Leschetizky felt he had known him personally. Leschetizky was given to making occasional provocative remarks of the kind: 'It is harder to play six bars well than to conduct the whole of the Ninth Symphony of Beethoven.'

Annette Hullah, *Theodor Leschetizky*, London and New York: J. Land & Co., 1906, p. 3.

FRANZ LISZT

As an interpreter, Franz Liszt may be regarded as being a direct descendant of Beethoven; he had been a pupil of Carl Czerny, who, in turn, as we have remarked (see above), learned Beethoven's sonatas directly from the composer. It was Liszt's championing of Beethoven's piano sonatas, especially in his early years as a concert pianist, which did much to raise them from their relative neglect and to place them at the forefront of the pianists' repertoire. We learn something of this from Liszt's own recollections.

In 1876 Liszt wrote of the period, from about 1821, when he commenced his studies with Carl Czerny. Liszt, like Czerny, was ten years old when he began his studies although even by then his remarkable powers were much in evidence — in fact Czerny complained that Liszt had learned too much too soon. Liszt tells us:

> 'Many of Beethoven's sonatas were known and profoundly admired, especially the *Pathétique*, *Moonlight* and *Appassionata*, but it wasn't the custom to play them in public. Not until after Beethoven's death did his works circulate everywhere.'

As recalled in: William S. Newman, *The Sonata in the Classic Era*, Chapel Hill: University of North Carolina Press 1963, pp. 528–9.

A measure of the aloofness, if not downright hostility, to Beethoven's later piano music is conveyed in an account from the writings of Beethoven's early biographer Wilhelm von Lenz. He has this to say of his experience of the reception of the composer's late piano sonatas when Liszt was performing them in Paris in the 1820s:

> 'The last five [Opp. 101, 106, 109, 110 and 111] passed for the monstrous abortions of a German idealist who did not know how to write for the piano. People only understood Hummel & Co.'

Derived from Harold C. Schonberg, *The Great Pianists*, London: Victor Gollancz, 1964, p. 92.

A further indication of the time it took for Beethoven's late piano music to reach the ears of even the musically informed, can be inferred from a diary entry of Giacomo Meyerbeer dating from 1862. He writes:

> 'With Cornelie [a friend] to Hans von Bülow's concert which was devoted to piano music [including] Beethoven's Sonata in A major, Op. 101 which I had never heard before, a gifted glorious work, particularly the first elegiac movement and the third or fourth, which is a fugue.'

In passing, we may observe that Hans von Bülow, now largely remembered as a conductor, was, together with Franz Liszt, a pioneer in promoting the awareness of

Beethoven's late piano sonatas to a wider public in the nineteenth century.

Robert Ignatius Letellier, editor and translator, *The Diaries of Giacomo Meyerbeer*, Madison: Fairleigh Dickinson University Press; London: Associated University Presses, 4 vols., 1999–2004, Vol. 4, p. 245.

In the autumn of 1839 Liszt gave a series of recitals in Vienna — he was twenty-eight at the time. Writing in the *Allgemeine Theaterzeitung* (30 November), the theatre and music critic Heinrch Adamai described Liszt's reception in the following terms:

> 'The enthusiasm which this great virtuoso is exciting in Vienna cannot be described ... No sooner is one of his concerts over than everyone is already longing for the next ... Not since Paganini has an artist made such a magical impression on the Viennese public.'

On 2 December, Liszt gave his third recital that included a performance of the *Appassionata* Sonata. Of this, Adamai wrote in the *Allgemeine Theaterzeitung* (4 December):

> 'Liszt began with the F minor Sonata of Beethoven [Op. 57]. The one which when played by Clara Schumann (see below) had given rise to such vehement debate in our newspapers ... For younger listeners in particular, who never had the opportunity of hearing Beethoven himself in his piano sonatas and concertos, Liszt's renderings are of exceptional interest, and from them are best able to study these works, often capable of so multifarious an interpretation, and to form a correct view for themselves.'

*

Liszt further demonstrated his remarkable powers on 5 December when he gave his fourth recital in Vienna's *Redoutensaal* — the 'fancy-dress' ballroom where Beethoven's Eighth Symphony was premiered. Liszt was billed to perform the composer's C minor Piano Concerto that was not then known to him. Despite feeling unwell, he learned the work and committed it to memory in a single day.

Adrian Williams, *Portrait of Liszt: By himself and his contemporaries*, Oxford: Clarendon Press, 1990, p. 115. An illustration of the interior of the *Redoutensaal*, where Beethoven had supplied music for the *Charity Ball* of 1795, is depicted in H. C. Robbins Landon, *Beethoven: A documentary study*, London: Thames and Hudson, 1970, p. 50, plate 33.

In his correspondence with the French writer George Sand, Liszt reveals how, in his youth, he would occasionally deceive an audience by passing off one of his own compositions as being by Beethoven. One such instance took place at a gathering of musical amateurs in Bordeaux in 1826 — Liszt was then fourteen years old. He played one of his own sonatas, telling them that it was by Beethoven. Liszt recalls how the assembly found the work to be "sublime". In Liszt's own words:

> 'I would play the same piece, presenting it at various times as one written by Beethoven, or by Czerny, or by myself ... At those times when I played it under Czerny's name, no one listened to me. But when I played it as a work of Beethoven, I could inevitably count on bravos from the entire hall.'

Franz Liszt, *An Artist's Journey: Lettres d'un bachelier dès musique, 1835–1841*, Chicago: University of Chicago Press, 1989.

Apart from revealing the prankish humour evident in Liszt's youthful personality, his anecdote illustrates how little known were Beethoven compositions, at the period in question, assisting the youthful prodigy to so deceive his audience.

In a letter to Dionys Pruckner, one of Liszt's piano pupils, Liszt recalled the piano playing of his teacher Carl Czerny. His brief observation casts light on Czerny's contribution to the promotion of Beethoven's works for piano:

> 'In the [eighteen] twenties, when a great portion of Beethoven's creations was a kind of Sphinx [the enigmatic Sphinx was at that period still largely shrouded in sand], Czerny was playing Beethoven *exclusively*, with an understanding as *excellent* as his technique was efficient and effective; and, later on, he did not set himself up against some progress that had been made in technique, but contributed materially to it by his own teaching and works.'

La Mara [pseudonym], *Letters of Franz Liszt*, London: H. Grevel & Co., 2 vols. 1894. Derived from Vol. 1, p. 266.

Several anecdotes connect Franz Liszt with Beethoven's C-sharp minor Piano Sonata, Op. 27, No. 2 *The Moonlight*. By all accounts Liszt, ever the dazzling virtuoso and lion of the keyboard, was occasionally willing to condone the taking of liberties with Beethoven's music — at least in his early years as a travelling virtuoso. For example, sometime around 1830 he gave a performance of the Op. 27, No. 2 Piano

Sonata to which he added 'trills and tremolos' and '*impassioned chords*' to the first movement. On another occasion he combined the first movement of the Op. 26 Sonata, which he played on the organ, with that of the final movement of *The Moonlight* that he played on the piano.

Derived from Alain Frogley in: Glen Stanley, editor, *The Cambridge Companion to Beethoven*, Cambridge; New York: Cambridge University Press, 2000, p. 24.

At a concert in Paris, in 1835, the first movement of the Op. 27, No. 2 Piano Sonata was performed in an arrangement for orchestra that Liszt then completed unaccompanied on the piano. The occasion was considered so memorable it was later depicted in various paintings and lithographs.

As recalled by William S. Newman, *The Sonata in the Classic Era*, Chapel Hill: University of North Carolina Press 1963, p. 518.

As Liszt's career as a virtuoso pianist progressed, so did his theatricality. Henry Reeve attended a recital given by Liszt when he was on a concert tour in Scotland in 1841; he performed in Glasgow and in Edinburgh's fashionable Assembly Rooms. Reeve was Editor of *The Edinburgh Review,* an intellectually inclined journal established in 1802 by men-of-letters — 'to gather all the rays of culture into one' (the journal's motto). Reeve's account of the Concert records the hall being very full and Liszt's person as being 'slight and tall, a delicate frame ... perpetually strained by the flow of animated thoughts'.

Liszt played a *Fantasia* of his own followed by Beethoven's C-sharp minor Piano Sonata. On completion of the Beethoven, Reeve took the platform, grasped Liszt's hand and 'thanked him for the divine energy that he had shed forth'. As the concert continued, as a consequence of the emotional stresses Liszt was suffering at the time — 'he fainted at the keyboard and had to be escorted from the hall'.

As recalled by Adrian Williams, *Portrait of Liszt: By himself and his contemporaries*, Oxford: Clarendon Press, 1990. Details of Liszt's concert tour in Scotland are described in, *Liszt Society Journal* 13 (1988) pp. 65–9. Liszt fainting at the keyboard is worthy of the Hollywood biographical film-romance *Song Without End: The Story of Franz Liszt*, in which the matinee idol Dirk Bogarde portrayed the celebrated pianist-composer.

The French dramatist Ernest Legouvé has left an account of the emotional effect Liszt's playing could have on individuals. The occasion in question was a private soirée attended by a small, but highly select, audience of connoisseurs. Legouvé describes how Liszt took his place at the piano and, as he puts it, 'began the funereal and heart-rending *Adagio* of the Sonata in C-sharp minor'. He himself was seated in an armchair and was disturbed by 'stifled sobs and moans'. He turned to look, only to see they came from non other than Hector Berlioz.

As recalled in: Alan Walker, *Franz Liszt, Volume 1, The virtuoso years: 1811-1847*, New York: Alfred A. Knopf, 1983, p. 182.

Incompetent playing by his pupils could upset Liszt's equanimity and he was given to describing wrong notes as 'uninvited guests'. His biographer Alan Walker relates: 'It was mainly in the defence of Beethoven and Bach that he would display the greatest aggression.'

A case in point occurred at a lesson in June 1882 – Liszt was then in his seventies. A young man had brought along a copy of the *Waldstein* Piano Sonata, Op. 53. Despite having received lessons from the distinguished pedagogue Theodor Kullak (himself a pupil of Liszt), he was inadequately prepared. His stumbling through the piece prompted Liszt to correct him at such frequent intervals that he finally flew into a rage, scattered the music and exclaimed:

'I do not take in washing here — do your washing at home!'

On another occasion the interpretation of a pupil who had just started to learn the *Waldstein* Piano Sonata also upset him; the young man's rhythm must have been all of a piece prompting Liszt to exclaim: 'Do not chop beefsteak for us!'

Alan Walker, *Franz Liszt, The final years, 1861–1886*, London: Faber and Faber, 1997, Volume 3, pp. 246–7.

Franz Liszt is usually accorded the honour of giving the first public performance of the Op. 106 Sonata in two recitals he performed in 1836 at the Salle Érard in Paris. There are many references to the early performances of the *Hammerklavier* Sonata by Franz Liszt; see for example: Edwin Fischer, 1959, p. 103 and Brian Rees, 1999, p. 29. Liszt himself tells us how he discovered the *Hammerklavier* Sonata at the unbelievably early age of ten. It is more probable that he 'played with' the Sonata rather than having performed it; nevertheless for a mere child to have the maturity of outlook to engage with such a work is remarkable. Of this, Liszt says:

> 'My father [his first teacher] wasn't up to it and Czerny [his subsequent teacher] was afraid to put me on such a diet.'

Adrian Williams, editor and translator, *Franz Liszt: Selected letters*, Oxford: Clarendon Press, 1998, p. 807.

A possible rival claimant to being the first to play the *Hammerklavier* Sonata, in public, is the Franco-Polish pianist Henri Mortier de Fontaine. History has now neglected him, but he is described in Grove's *A Dictionary of Music and Musicians* (1900) as being 'possessed of unusual technical ability'.

De Fontaine was born in Warsaw in 1816. If we assume he performed the *Hammerklavier* Piano Sonata sometime, say, in the early 1830s, he must still have been only in his late teens.

Alan Tyson, *The Authentic English Editions of Beethoven*, London: Faber and Faber, 1963, p. 105. The reader is also referred to the website text *Henri Mortier de Fontaine* for an account of this remarkable artist's life and work.

An anecdote from the recollections of the American pianist Amy Fay (1844–1928) connects us with Franz Liszt and the European musical scene of the 1870s. Fay was an accomplished performer who had travelled to Europe to study with Liszt; she also had lessons with two other lions of the keyboard, namely Theodor Kullak and Carl Tausig. On 19 June 1873 she heard a young student from Stuttgart perform the *Appassionata* Sonata for Liszt. Her Diary entry reveals the impression the music made upon her — and that of Liszt's interventions:

> '[The student] had a good deal of technique, and a moderately good conception of the work ... It was a hot afternoon, and the clouds had been gathering for a storm. As the Stuggarter played the opening notes, the tree tops suddenly waved wildly, and a low growl of thunder was heard muttering in the distance.'

Fay adds that, with the storm breaking, Liszt remarked with his characteristic alacrity: 'Ah, a fitting accompaniment!'

It appears though that Liszt was not impressed by the student's performance; he interrupted him at intervals and played passages himself, prompting Fay to record in her diary how magnificent was the little he did play and how startling was the individuality of his conception. She was so transported by the experience she later wrote: 'I did not know whether I were in the body or out of the body.'

Amy Fay, *Music-study in Germany: From the home correspondence of Amy Fay* [1880], New York: Dover Publications (reprint), 1965, pp. 229–30. See also: Adrian Williams, *Portrait of Liszt: By himself and his contemporaries,* Oxford: Clarendon Press, 1990, pp. 496–7.

Reflecting late in life on his relationship with the piano, Liszt remarked:

> 'My piano ... is to me what his frigate is to the sailor, his charger to the Arab; even more perhaps, for my piano has been until now my very self, my words, my life; it is the intimate repository of everything that stirred and tossed within my mind during the most ardent days of my youth; all my desires, dreams, joys, and sorrows were found in it. Its strings have shuddered under my passions, its submissive keys obeyed my every whim ... Perhaps I am deceived by this kind of mysterious feeling which attaches me to the piano, yet I consider its importance very great. It has, it seems to me, the leading place in the hierarchy of instruments. It is the most generally cultivated, the most popular of all; and this importance and this popularity it owes in part to the harmonic power which it alone possesses; and, as a consequence of this power, to the faculty of summarizing and concentrating within itself the whole of the art of music. In the span of seven octaves it embraces the range of an orchestra; and ten fingers of man suffice to render the harmonies produced by the

concourse of more than a hundred instruments put together.'

Adrian Williams, *Portrait of Liszt: By himself and his contemporaries*, Oxford: Clarendon Press, 1990, pp. 92–3.

WITOLD LUTOSLOVWSKI

In conversation with the Russian musicologist Irina Nikolska, Witold Lutoslovwski reflected on the value of the Beethoven studies he had taken with his namesake Witold Maliszewski, professor of piano at the Warsaw Conservatoire:

> 'My teacher knew how to analyse Beethoven's sonatas proceeding from the psychological aspect of musical form, utterly rejected by the most authoritative German experts in music theory, who regarded this method of approach as 'unscientific'.

Lutoslovwski continues:

> 'Maliszewski distinguished between four "characters" (i.e., types of musical utterance): introductory, narrative, transitional, and concluding ... Professor Maliszewski corroborated these theses by analysing Beethoven's sonatas. Indeed, in Beethoven thematic material proper — a new musical thought, that is to say, a new theme, — always appears in "narrative" sections, whereas in "transitional-natured" episodes use is made, as a rule, of frequently recurring motives taken out of the theme(s), with numerous modulations making

for an intensive harmonic development. Also in introductory and concluding sections, form is more important than thematic content. An introduction, for example, is supposed to suggest to the listener that some significant events are expected to take place before long — they are to take place before long, but are not yet taking place at the moment.'

Irina Nikolska, *Conversations with Witold Lutoslovwski (1987–92),* Stockholm: Melos, 1994, p. 89.

EDWARD MACDOWELL

In his essay on the development of piano music, the American composer and pianist Edward MacDowell comments:

'We find that Beethoven was the first exponent of our modern art. Every revolution is bound to bring with it a reaction which seeks to consolidate and put in safe keeping, as it were, results attained by it. We may say then broadly that Beethoven invested instrumental music with a wonderful poignancy and power of expression, elevating it to the point of being the medium of expressing some of the greatest thoughts we possess. In so doing, however, he shattered many of the great idols of formalism by the sheer violence of his expression.'

Edward MacDowell, *Critical and Historical Essays: Lectures delivered at Columbia University,* edited by W. J. Baltzell, London: Elkin; Boston: A.P. Schmidt, 1912, p. 203.

GUSTAV MAHLER

As a student Gustav Mahler heard Anton Rubinstein perform the complete cycle of Beethoven piano sonatas in Vienna and later in Leipzig and Hamburg. One of these series of concerts was spent in the company of the viola player, and devoted admirer of Mahler, Natalie Bauer-Lechner. She has left this reminiscence of that occasion:

> 'We began to talk about the playing of Beethoven's sonatas. Mahler said that this is particularly difficult because the sonata demands a freer, more improvisational style of performance than that of orchestral works. The latter have a firm structure; they are already held together by the necessary interaction of all the various instruments.'

Concerning Rubinstein's interpretation of Beethoven, Bauer-Lechner adds:

> '[Mahler] called Rubinstein a "man of the Steppes" ... by which he meant to indicate the elemental force, the boundless power and lack of cultivation — in the sense of nature, which needs no cultivation — of that magnificent artist.'

Natalie Bauer-Lechner, *Recollections of Gustav Mahler*, London: Faber Music, 1980, p.174.

DENNIS MATTHEWS

The British pianist and musicologist Dennis Matthews made a study of Beethoven's piano sonatas for the British Broadcasting Corporation. The following is an extract:

'Think for a moment of the variety of [Beethoven's] sonatas and the width of their appeal. Even the most casual of music-lovers has been known to succumb to the strange, veiled potency of the first movement of the so-called *Moonlight*. Is there a general-practising virtuoso who escapes carrying either the *Waldstein* or *Appassionata* in his repertoire? (And what companion works could be more different in their affirmation of major and minor keys?) The intellectual who confesses, to his loss, that middle-period Beethoven has nothing new to say to him will still turn to the *Hammerklavier* as one of the stiffest challenges for player and listener alike; yet for those who fight shy of the epic, titanic Beethoven there are sonatas in all periods that converse in intimate domestic tones. Even the youngest pianists can still find an entrance to Beethoven's world through the sonatas. As they mature in mind and fingers they may set their sights on the lofty pinnacles of the late works; but they will be constantly surprised at the unsuspected richness of the earlier slow movements. "Early", however, needs some qualification in Beethoven's case. He wrote three childhood sonatas in his Bonn days which are prophetic, maybe, but are not normally accepted into the self-approved cannon. [This is a reference to the so-called *Kurfürstensonaten Sonatas* that Beethoven composed between the ages of twelve and thirteen that he dedicated to the Elector (Kurfüst) Maximillian Frederick.] Beethoven was twenty-five when he confirmed his readiness by publishing works with opus-numbers, a late-starter by Mozartean standards.'

Dennis Matthews, *Beethoven, Piano Sonatas*, London: British Broadcasting Corporation, 1967, p. 5.)

Of Beethoven in relation to the piano Matthews writes.

'Beethoven had watched the growing scope of the piano and utilized its resources to the utmost — beyond the utmost at times. Yet he can hardly be called a pioneer of piano technique in the sense that Chopin, or even Clementi and Czerny, were pioneers. The piano was a means to an end, not to be wooed for its own sake but a vehicle for expression — to be bullied, if necessary, into submission. There is scarcely a passage in Beethoven, early or late, that could be modified in the interests of technique, comfort or "effectiveness" without dissipation of the strength and willpower that made it. The artist thrives within his limitations and even the much-worked Alberti bass and the routine range of arpeggio formulas served Beethoven well.'

In Matthews' opinion Beethoven was not strictly a 'harmonic composer':

'Neither could Beethoven be called a harmonic composer in the normal sense — in many instances Mozart was much more "modern" in his use of dissonance — and his frequent reliance on tonic-and-dominant patterns, on Neapolitan sixths and diminished sevenths, has been ridiculed by those who obstinately refuse to see the wood for the trees. Wherein lies his extraordinary strength, then? The answer lies in Beethoven's unique mastery of tonality and key relationships, the larger view of harmony; or, putting it another way, in the architectural sense he could find more resources in the deployment of ordinary structural bricks than less enduring, though more alluring, decorative ones. Only a short-sighted view can find a commonplace in the *Waldstein*.'

Dennis Matthews, *Keyboard Music*, Newton Abbot: London David & Charles, 1972, pp. 181–2.

Concerning performance from memory, Matthews remarks:

'The tradition of playing from memory is comparatively recent and according to historians little more than a century old, but it is now almost a hard and fast rule that pianists in particular should habitually dispense with the music in public; and so expected is this feat that a rustle of disappointment can be heard running through the audience if the player brings the notes and a turn-over on the platform with him ... Reliance on memory may limit the repertoire, cramp the musicianship, and at its worst lead to sins of varying nature against the score.'

Dennis Matthews, *In Pursuit of Music*, London: Victor Gollancz Ltd., 1968, pp. 132–3.

*

WILFRID MELLERS

The English musicologist and composer Wilfrid Mellers considers Beethoven's piano sonatas in their social and psychological context:

> 'Beethoven's "process" is religious as well as social, for his sonata forms, especially in later years, seek an undivided whole. One might say that for Bach music was a religious rite, for Mozart a social activity, and for Beethoven a psychological event.'

Wilfrid Mellers, *Between Old Worlds and New: Occasional writings on music*, in: John Paynter, editor, London: Cygnus Arts, 1997, p. 16.

OLIVIER MESSIAN

The French journalist and music critic Claude Samuel interviewed Olivier Messian and asked him the question: 'Where does your passion for teaching come from?'

Messian replied:

> '[T]eaching for me has always had a dual purpose: it has allowed me to come to the aid of young composers who were seeking direction and, at the same time, to complete my education by analysing scores sometimes very foreign to me. And I've always loved musical analysis; curiously, it was while in captivity that I acquired a taste for it. [In 1940 Messian was imprisoned in Stalag.] A German officer gave me an edition of Beethoven's piano scores as a gift. Since my childhood, I had pored over the composition

treatise of Vincent d'Indy and his commentaries on Beethoven and sonata form, so I was well prepared to read these sonatas closely, and I recognised them as the miracles of structure that they are.'

Olivier Messian, *Music and Color: Conversations with Claude Samuel*, Portland, Oregon: Amadeus, 1994, p. 175.

WILLIAM S. NEWMAN

The American musicologist William S. Newman writing about Beethoven's piano sonatas in the classical era remarks:

'Beethoven's piano sonatas span forty years of his life (1782–1822). More than any other category of his music, they give a rounded view of his styles and forms throughout his creative periods. Furthermore, unlike the keyboard sonatas of Haydn and Mozart, they have generally been ranked among the most important works in the total production of their creator.'

William S. Newman, *The Sonata in the Classic Era*, New York; London: W.W. Norton, 1983, p. 507.

CARL NIELSEN

In 1906 Carl Nielsen was commissioned to write an essay to mark the 150th anniversary of the birth of Mozart. Notwithstanding that Mozart was his subject, Nielsen found space to make a passing reference to Beethoven — not entirely complementary:

'From Beethoven, one learns to build an *allegro* movement, with its two themes and modulation section. But it is remarkable that this master — music's greatest lyricist — is strict, yes, often stiff and unyielding in his form.'

Mina Miller, *The Nielsen Companion*, London: Faber and Faber, 1994, p. 71.

HUBERT PARRY

Sir Charles Hubert Hastings Parry was a former pillar of the English musical establishment, occupying the professorship in music at the University of Oxford and later the headship of the Royal College of Music where his pupils included Vaughn Williams, Gustav Holst, Frank Bridge and John Ireland. From his substantial musical output, Parry is best remembered today for his choral song *Jerusalem* and his setting for the coronation anthem 'I was glad when they said unto me'.

In his undergraduate days at Oxford, Parry was co-founder of *The Music Club* and it was at this period when Beethoven's pianos sonatas 'cast a powerful spell' upon him. His Diary for 27 December 1866 records: 'Practised all morning — Beethoven mostly'.

The work he studied intently was the Piano Sonata in F, Op. 10, No. 2. When Parry succeeded Sir Charles Grove as Director of the Royal College of Music, of necessity he devoted much of his time to college administration but not to the neglect of composition and musicology. In the latter capacity he published a study of Beethoven (1886) that containing an evaluation of his works, including the piano sonatas. In this he writes: 'The imagination and the reason must both be satisfied, but above all things the imagination.'

C. Hubert H. Parry, *Beethoven* in: David Ewen, *From Bach to Stravinsky: The history of music by its foremost critics*, New York, Greenwood Press, 1968, pp. 105–131.

Aware that his technique in piano had many shortcomings, Parry took lessons from his music teacher Professor James Taylor — remembered today for establishing Oxford's chamber music recitals. According to Parry's Diary (27 December 1866) 'Taylor soon had him tackling the Op, 57 Piano Sonata — the *Appassionata*.'

Writing of Parry's student days, Anthony Boden recalls:

> 'He had discovered the music of Beethoven and begun to explore the sonatas, and with Taylor's guidance was soon scaling the peaks of the *Appassionata*, but only after the ending of the Trinity term would the full impact of Beethoven's genius take him like a flood.'

It was at this period that Parry heard Beethoven's Fifth Symphony for the first time, prompting him to enthuse:

> 'Words cannot express the hopeless gloriousness of this old ruffian! Such a whacker! So tremendously massive!'

Parry was to put his knowledge of the *Appassionata* to good effect years later when he guided his young protégé Vaughn Williams through his own music studies. In his estimation of the Op. 57 Piano Sonata Parry wrote the moving words: 'Here the human soul asked mighty questions of its God and had its reply.'

And of the composer more generally he remarked:

> '[Beethoven] is one of the few great creators of
> art whom a man, though he be ever so blessed
> with musical intelligence, may study for a lifetime
> and never exhaust.'

Jeremy C. Dibble, *Hubert H. Parry: His life and music*, Oxford: Clarendon Press, 1992, pp. 50–1 and Anthony Boden, *The Parrys of the Golden Vale: Background to genius*, London: Thames Publishing, 1998, 120–1.

MENAHAN PRESSLER

Musicologist Nicholus Delbanco asked Menahan Pressler, the pianist member of the *Beaux Arts Trio*, if he considered the performer should learn the early piano sonatas of Beethoven first, given how radically his work changed over the course of time. Pressler replied:

> 'Yes, some of them. Few of us have time to learn
> all the early sonatas. You should progress in this
> way, of course, from early to late. If you were to
> start right off with the late ones, it would be like
> reading a book in a foreign language in such a
> way that you had to look up every word with a
> dictionary in one hand and the book in the other.
> You must know the ABCs first ... Then, in the
> later work, [Beethoven's] soul became rarefied.
> These works seem to express philosophical
> concepts besides the sound, besides the tech-
> nique of their composition, but also as a man. I
> love to play them for what I know they can do to
> others, and I love to teach them because of what
> they can open up in a student. Younger artists
> may not have the capacity for seeing and under-

standing these works, but that is what we strive for. That is what these works demand: to see ever more clearly, more deeply, without ever stopping, without ever being really satisfied.'

Nicholas Delbanco, *The Beaux Arts Trio*, London: Gollancz, 1985, p. 171.

SERGEI PROKOFIEV

Reflecting on his early piano lessons Prokofiev recalls:

> '[T]here was always music in the home ... When I was put to bed at night, I never wanted to sleep. I would lie there and listen as the sound of a Beethoven sonata came from somewhere far off, several rooms away. More than anything else, my mother played the sonatas of Volume I.'

Prokofiev soon commenced piano lessons and by the age of five composed his first piano composition — written down by his mother. By the age of eleven, Prokofiev received piano instruction from the distinguished Soviet composer, conductor, and teacher Reinhold Glière. Of this period he writes:

> 'A born teacher, Glière skillfully combined instruction in harmony with free composition and a study of the elements of form and orchestration ... Playing a Beethoven sonata Glière would give me a rough outline of sonata form, and whenever we came across a phrase characteristic of one or another instrument in a symphony orchestra, he would say: "Now this melody could be played by

> a flute; the fanfare could be given to the trumpet, and in the lower register to two French horns", etc.'

An anecdote from Prokofiev's memoirs is of related interest. At the age of fourteen he was a student at the Conservatory at St. Petersburg and wished to be considered for entry to the 'special piano class' – an endeavour known to be very demanding. His teacher at the time was Alexander Winkler who asked his youthful protégé if he knew Beethoven's Piano Sonata Op. 22. 'By heart', was Prokofiev's reply. He subsequently performed the piece before eight or nine examiners – 'all grim-faced' – but, two hours later, they told him he was accepted. Winkler's response was to say:

> 'To start with we'll work on techniques to strengthen your fingers. It'll be a bit boring at first, but there's nothing we can do about it.'

Sergey Prokofiev, *Prokofiev by Prokofiev: A composer's memoir*, London: Macdonald and Jane's, 1979, pp. 89–90.

Later in his mature years Prokofiev wrote:

> '[The] thinking of one and the same composer can be both complex and simple. Take the second volume of the piano sonatas [of Beethoven]. No one would go so far as to claim that the simple sonatas in that volume are better or more necessary than the complex ones.'

Christopher Palmer, editor, *Sergei Prokofiev: Soviet diary 1927 and other writings*, London: Faber and Faber, 1991, p. 23, p. 232 and p. 286.

*

SVIATOSLAV RICHTER

The American pianist and author David Dubal recalls the impression the Soviet pianist Sviatoslav Richter conveyed when playing Beethoven:

> 'Sviatoslav Richter strides out on the stage. His face is grim; there is anger in the set jaw, but not at the audience. This is a passion altogether his own, a force with which he protects what he is about to do ... Now he begins to play, and the anger I see in his bearing I hear in the voice of Beethoven. It knows nothing of meanness or spite; it is the passion of the doer who will not let his work be swept aside. It hurts no one, it asserts life, it is the force that generates form.'

Alexander Coleman, editor, *Diversions & Animadversions: Essays from The new criterion*, New Brunswick, New Jersey; London: Transaction Publishers, 2005, p. 172.

Richter explained his approach to performance as follows:

> 'The interpreter is really an executant, carrying out the composer's intentions to the letter. He doesn't add anything that isn't already in the work. If he is talented, he allows us to glimpse the truth of the work that is in itself a thing of genius and that is reflected in him. He shouldn't dominate the music, but should dissolve into it.'

Bruno Monsaingeon, Sviatoslav *Richter: Notebooks and conversations*, Princeton University Press, 2001, p. 153.

*

FERDINAND RIES

The German composer and pianist Ferdinand Ries was a pupil of Beethoven from 1801 to 1804, the period when he made his public debut as a concert pianist playing the composer's C minor Piano Concerto, Op. 37 — with his own cadenza. In 1838 Ries published a collection of reminiscences of Beethoven, co-written with the composer's life-long friend the distinguished physician Franz Wegeler. These appeared under the original title *Biographische Notizen über Ludwig van Beethoven* and are considered to be an important and reliable source of information. They are available in English as: Franz Wegeler, *Remembering Beethoven: The biographical notes of Franz Wegeler and Ferdinand Ries*, London: Andre Deutsch, 1988.

Perhaps the most repeated anecdote told about Ries does not concern the piano sonatas but relates to the occasion of the first rehearsal of the *Eroica* Symphony. During this, Ries mistakenly believed the horn player had come in too early and said so to Beethoven — incurring his displeasure. It is also from Ferdinand Ries we learn of the deterioration of Beethoven's hearing. When out walking in the countryside one day Ries heard a shepherd playing his pipe — possibly a shawm. It was apparent to him that Beethoven was quite unaware of its sound and so discreetly made out that he too could not hear anything.

Recalling his days in Vienna, when he received piano instruction from Beethoven, Ries states:

> 'If I missed something in a passage, or played wrongly the notes and leaps he often wanted me to bring out strongly, he rarely said anything; but when I fell short as regards expression, crescendos, etc., or the character of the piece, he got exasperated because he said, the first was an

accident, but the other was a lack of judgement, feeling or attentiveness. The former happened to him quite often too, even when he played in public.'

Wegeler-Ries, 1988, p. 94 et seq. See also Ferdinand Ries cited in: Alfred Brendel, *Alfred Brendel on Music: Collected essays*, Chicago, Iliinois: A Cappella Books, 2001, p. 48.

Despite his fiery temperament, Ries's recollections suggest Beethoven was a patient teacher. Writing to the publisher Nikolous Simrock, Ries remarks:

'Beethoven takes more pains with me than I shall ever have believed possible. 'I have three lessons a week, usually from one o'clock till half past two.'

It is at this period that Ries studied the *Pastoral* Sonata, Op. 28 with the composer that he later transcribed for string quartet.

For an account of Ferdinand Ries and his relationship with Beethoven, see: Peter Clive, *Beethoven and his World*, Oxford University Press, 2001, p. 285.

Ries left the following account of Beethoven's style at the piano:

'In general he played his own compositions in a very capricious manner, but he nevertheless kept strictly accurate time, occasionally, but very seldom, accelerating the tempo. On the other hand, in the performance of a crescendo passage, he would introduce a retard, which produced a beautiful and highly striking effect. Sometimes, in

> the performance of specific passages, he would
> infuse into them an exquisite but altogether inim-
> itable expression. He seldom introduced notes or
> ornaments not set down in the composition.'

Ferdinand Ries cited in: Harold C. Schonberg, *The Great Pianists*, London: Victor Gollancz, 1964, p. 78. See also: Hans Conrad Fischer and Erich Kock, *Ludwig van Beethoven: A study in text and pictures*, London: Macmillan; New York, St. Martin's Press, 1972, p. 14.

A possible source of influence on Beethoven, in deciding to include a funeral march in his Piano Sonata Op. 26, may have been the opera *Achilles* by the composer Ferdinand (Ferdinando) Paer. This work, a melodrama, celebrates the central character Achilles, Homer's renowned hero of the Trojan Wars. It was premiered on 6 June 1801 at the *Kärntnertor-Theater* where Paer was then Music Director. Writing about this Ries states:

> 'The Funeral March in A-flat minor in the sonata
> dedicated to Prince Lichnowsky (Opus 26) orig-
> inated in the great praise Paer's funeral march in
> his opera *Achilles* received from Beethoven's
> friends.'

Carl Czerny, who had become a pupil of Beethoven at the time of the premiere of *Achilles*, also makes brief mention of Paer's opera with regard to Beethoven's Op. 26. It is probable Beethoven did not have a particular hero in mind for the subject of his Funeral March; doubtless he was intent upon giving more generalised musical expression to the feelings of loss associated with mourning.

Wegeler-Ries, 1988, p. 70.

Sometime late in 1806, Ries felt an obligation to acknowledge the debt he felt he owed to his teacher and duly wrote to Beethoven informing him of his intention to dedicate to him his own two Piano Sonatas Op. 1:

> 'I shall take this occasion to express my gratitude to you publically; the sincere and the more ardent for the intimacy that you have allowed me, and for the friendship with which you have honoured me. The memory of pleasant hours spent near you will never fade from my heart, and if my efforts are rewarded by any success, it is to your counsel that I shall be indebted.'

Derived from Theodore Albrecht, translator and editor, *Letters to Beethoven and other Correspondence*, Lincoln, New England: University of Nebraska Press, 1996, Vol. 1, Letter No. 121, pp. 189–90.

Ries played an important role in establishing Beethoven's works in England, particularly in connection with the Philharmonic Society of London — later the Royal Philharmonic Society. He took up residence in London in April 1813 and was elected a director of the Society two years later. He was active in the promotion of his own compositions that included eight piano concertos, eight symphonies and 26 string quartets. These works reveal a style, not unsurprisingly, owning a debt to his teacher. Ries maintained contact with Beethoven to the end and was instrumental (no pun intended) in bringing before the English public several of Beethoven's piano sonatas and other compositions. Perhaps Ries's most significant contribution in this context was the role he played, in 1822, in the Philharmonic Society's commissioning of Beethoven's Choral Symphony.

ROMAIN ROLLAND

Notwithstanding his celebrity as a philosopher, dramatist, novelist, essayist, art historian and Nobel Laureate (prize for literature in 1915) Romain Rolland wrote extensively on music and was appointed to the first chair of music history at the Sorbonne in 1903. His passion for music — he was an accomplished pianist — found expression in several studies of Beethoven who for Rolland was 'the universal musician above all the others'.

His writings about the composer and his works include: *Beethoven and Handel* (1917); *Goethe and Beethoven* (1930); and *Beethoven the Creator* (1937). His *Essays on Music* (1915) also include a study of Beethoven's thirtieth year.

In his survey of Beethoven's piano sonatas, he classified them in the order he considered suitable to their study. The following is the sequence he lists:

Op. 49 No. 2	Op. 31 No. 1
Op. 49 No. 1	Op. 31 No. 3
Op. 14 No. 2	Op. 90
Op. 14 No. 1	Op. 54
Op. 79	Op. 27 No. 1
Op. 2 No. 1	Op. 27 No. 2 *Moonlight*
Op. 10 No. 1	Op. 31 No. 2
Op. 10 No. 2	Op. 53
Op. 10 No. 3	Op. 81 *Les Adieux*
Op. 13 *Pathétique*	Op. 78
Op. 22	Op. 57 *Appassionata*
Op. 28 *Pastorale*	Op. 110
Op. 2 No. 2	Op. 109
Op. 2 No. 3	Op. 101
Op. 7	Op. 111
Op. 26	Op. 106 *Hammerklavier*

Romain Rolland, *Beethoven and Handel*. London: Waverley Book Co., 1917, pp. 209–10.

CHARLES ROSEN

The American pianist and musicologist Charles Rosen made an intensive study of Beethoven's piano sonatas and their interpretation from which the following extracts are derived:

> 'The pianistic repertoire supplied by the Beethoven sonatas was one of the principal causes of the shift of the balance of music-making from the private house to the public hall. Intended for the more intimate surroundings, many of the sonatas were seen to be wonderfully apt for virtuoso performance in large halls. Some of the earliest sonatas already presented difficulties resented by the average amateur, and the technical obstacles became harder to surmount with the "Waldstein", the "Appassionata", and "Les Adieux". Later still, it was the "Hammerklavier", Op. 106, which appeared to shut out the amateur completely. "There is a lady in Vienna", Czerny told Beethoven, "who has been practising your B-flat Sonata for a month, and still can't play the beginning." Nevertheless, most of the sonatas remained just within the grasp of the amateur who could still make something of them: their difficulties, indeed, gave a sense of contact, however tenuous, with the professional that one could get from almost no other set of serious works. They were a challenge which could be taken on, an ideal to which one could aspire, even if they could not in the end be fully mastered — not even, as Artur Schnabel remarked, by the consummate professional: "no performance of a Beethoven sonata", he claimed, "could be as great as the work itself".'

*

Concerning Beethoven's expression marks, Rosen states:

> 'The changes in phrasing and touch [in Beethoven's sonatas] are integral to the scenario, the concentration of dramatic development. We can find precedents for Beethoven's procedures, particularly in the early work of Haydn, but the transformations of a musical idea by touch, dynamics and phrasing had never been seen before Beethoven on such a scale or with such concentrated intensity. Nor was it ever seen again. This is one of the many reasons the sonatas remain so fascinating to play.'

Concerning tempo Rosen remarks:

> 'It is not illegal to play a piece of music at the wrong tempo: we risk neither a jail sentence nor even a fine. A certain school of aesthetics considers it immoral to contravene the composer's intentions, but sometimes it may even be a good idea. We have all heard performances at clearly inauthentic and even absurd tempos which turn out to be revealing, instructive, moving or brilliantly effective. The wrong tempo might be still more effective than the right one. This leads some musicians to conclude that there is no correct tempo, and this may be true for certain styles of music in some periods. Nevertheless, Beethoven evidently thought there was a right tempo for each of his works, although it is not entirely clear that he himself always knew or had correctly decided on what that tempo should be.'

*

Rosen concludes:

> 'It is a fundamental mistake to think that a tempo with which we are comfortable today is bound to be correct. Instruments have changed, concert halls are different, habits of listening have altered. Sensibilities have changed as well. It is true that the majority of tempos at which we now perform Beethoven raise few problems. However, when we study the way Beethoven employed tempo indications, there will be some surprises. We have a bad habit of dismissing a tempo which goes against the grain which makes us ill at ease — claiming that Beethoven must be in error, or that a copyist was at fault. If, like all composers, Beethoven did on rare occasions make mistakes, we would always need some evidence to be able to claim this — an instinctive reaction is not enough.'

Charles Rosen, *Beethoven's Piano Sonatas: A short companion*, New Haven; Connecticut: London: Yale University Press, 2002, pp. 6–7, p.41 and p. 43.

Elsewhere Rosen comments:

> 'There are moments when Beethoven is as chromatic as any composer before late Wagner, including Chopin, but the chromaticism is always resolved and blended into a background which ends by leaving the tonic triad absolute master.'

Charles Rosen, *The Classical Style: Haydn, Mozart, Beethoven*, London: Faber and Faber, 1976, p. 387.

Concerning modern-day performance on period instruments, Rosen comments:

> 'Above all, playing the ancient instruments with their weaker, subtle, and more fragile tone in a large space with modern acoustics only exacerbates the problem of revealing the music to the public. Reviving the sonority of an eighteenth-century piano is defeated when it is played in a hall that seats more than two or three hundred people even when it is completely audible, which is not always the case: it may be the same instrument, but it is not at all the same sound. Recordings are a more successful means of transmission, but more than anything else, the emphasis on the recorded performance has only reinforced the modern delusion that music is intended more for listening than playing. Nevertheless, the "Authenticity" movement has been salutary and beneficial. Few pianists today would want to perform a Beethoven sonata without at least taking into account the sonority it might have had during the composer's time.'

Charles Rosen, *Critical Entertainments: Music old and new,* Cambridge, Massachusetts; London: Harvard University Press, 2000, p. 300.

When asked if he felt the urge to perform on the fortepiano, Rosen replied: 'No. I don't really find that attractive at all; basically it seems to me that most composers' imaginations — Beethoven's particularly — always exceed the instruments of their time. In one respect a fortepiano is a kind of fraud because one assumes there was a kind of instrument in the eighteenth century called the fortepiano which had a certain sound. But in fact there were lots of different types of fortepianos, each having different kinds of sounds. A Viennese piano was so different from an English piano of the time that you might as well have given them different names. Certainly Beethoven expected his music to be played on a great variety of pianos and the music was intended to meet that requirement ... For instance, there are passages in Beethoven which are easier to play on an old piano, while other passages don't "come off" on the old piano at all. Beethoven must have known what would work and what wouldn't, but he still wanted to write them. In other words, there are advantages to both. On the whole, I think the balance is in favour of the modern piano, particularly since the old pianos only work in halls that seat less than 200 people, and you can't make a living playing to audiences of that kind anymore.'

Charles Rosen in conversation with the pianist and musicologist David Dubal in, David Dubal, *The World of the Concert Pianist,* London: Victor Gollancz, 1985, p. 274.

Discussing the last sonatas, Rosen states:

> 'The last sonatas are more radical ... as if the writing of Op. 106 had given Beethoven new confidence. The experimental works of the preceding years shared some of the ideals of Beethoven's younger contemporaries; they were close to the music of the next generation, above all the works of Schumann and Mendelssohn. The increase in Beethoven's deafness made him withdraw into himself in greater isolation. The last piano sonatas needed a much longer time to enter the mainstream of musical influence. Even

> the last quartets were easier for later composers to assimilate.'

We conclude our selection of extracts from Rosen's writings with his observations:

> 'For all the consternation that the works of the middle period had aroused in critics and musicians, the Sonatas of Op. 31 and the *Waldstein* and *Appassionata*, revealed themselves fairly quickly to be respectable concert pieces. They are deeply serious works, but they do not seem to have, at first hearing, the forthright moral earnestness of the sonatas from the *Pathétique* to *Les Adieux*, largely because they make few concessions to the listener. Understanding them, taking pleasure in hearing them, requires an active participation from the listener never demanded before from the piano sonata. They have understandably inspired a good deal of pretentious interpretation in both writing and performance. This was inevitable: the composer clearly intended these works as exemplars of great spiritual experience. It is less evident that Beethoven's ideas of transcendence is the same as ours.'

Charles Rosen, *Beethoven's Piano Sonatas: A short companion*, New Haven, Connecticut: London: Yale University Press, 2002, p. 229.

ANTON RUBINSTEIN
The Russian born Anton Rubinstein is regarded as one of the foremost keyboard virtuosos of the nineteenth century.

His contemporary Hans von Bülow, himself a pianist of formidable accomplishments, described him as *The Michelangelo of Music* and the German music critic Ludwig Rellstab was equally fulsome in his praise of Rubinstein, calling him *The Hercules of the Piano*.

Harold C. Schonberg, *The Great Pianists*, Simon & Schuster, 1963, p. 269.

Rubinstein's contemporaries were struck by his physical resemblance to Beethoven. His virtuosity at the keyboard also called to mind that of Beethoven when he was at the height of his powers. It was said that when Liszt went on recital in Paris, every Érard piano was heard to grown and when Rubinstein performed they would erupt volcanically! Audiences were known to leave after one of Rubinstein's recitals in a state of near mental exhaustion as though they had experienced a force of nature. In these recitals he promoted Beethoven's piano sonatas that included programmes of formidable length and pianistic challenge. For example, on one occasion he played the *Moonlight, Tempest, Waldstein, Appassionata*, the A major (Op. 101) the E major (Op. 109) and the C minor Op. 111.

Harold C. Schonberg, op. cit., pp. 274–6.

The Belgian violinist and all-round musician Eugène Ysaÿe – known in his day as *The God of the Violin* – heard Rubinstein perform during a house party sometime in 1876 at which none other than Liszt was also a guest. Writing of Rubinstein's playing, Ysaÿe comments:

> 'He was truly my master of interpretation ... His power over the piano is something undreamt of; he transports you into another world; all that is mechanical in the instrument is forgotten. I am still under the influence of the all-embracing harmony, the scintillating passages and the

> thunder of Beethoven's Sonata Op. 57, which
> Rubinstein executed for us with unimagined
> mastery.'

Antoine Ysaÿe, *Ysaÿe: His life, Work and Influence*, London: W. Heinemann, 1947, p. 24.

Ten years later, it was the turn of Sergei Rachmaninoff — renowned for his own pianistic attainments — to have occasion to be captivated by Rubinstein's playing. Recalling his student days, from the period January–February 1886, Rachmaninoff informs us that Rubinstein was alternating between St. Petersburg and Moscow giving recitals. Rachmaninoff was so in thrall to the legendary interpreter of Beethoven that he heard him perform as often as he could. He enthuses:

> 'It was less his magnificent technique that held one spellbound than the profound, spiritually refined musicianship that sounded from each work he played. I remember how deeply I was affected by his playing of Beethoven's *Appassionata*, and Chopin's Sonata in B flat minor.'

On one such occasion Rubinstein was so dissatisfied with his rendering of the short closing crescendo in the Chopin Sonata he promptly repeated the entire work.

Sergei Rachmaninoff, *Rachmaninoff's Recollections told to Oskar von Riesemann*, London: George Allen & Unwin, 1934, pp. 12–3.

It was during one of his visits to Paris that Rubinstein heard the French Pianist Alfred Cortot play the first movement of the *Appassionata* Piano Sonata. Cortot's interpretation did not please Rubinstein, disposing him to proclaim the maxim by which he himself approached the composer's music:

> 'My boy, don't you ever forget what I am going to tell you. Beethoven's music must not be studied. It must be reincarnated.'

Schonberg op. cit., p. 406.

ARTHUR RUBINSTEIN

The Polish-American pianist Arthur Rubinstein is universally admired and remembered for being one of the greatest interpreters of the music of Frédéric Chopin. However, his repertoire embraced works by many other composers including Beethoven. Rubinstein's recollections of his student days connect us to the Piano Sonata Op. 106 and give a hint of his views of the music and his thoughts about its performance.

In the summer of 1910, when he was twenty-three years old, Rubinstein took part in a piano competition held in St. Petersburg; it was named in honour of his namesake, the great Beethovenian Anton Rubinstein. Notwithstanding Rubinstein's endeavours, the first prize went to a fellow student by the name of Alfred Hoehn. Rubinstein generously acknowledged Hoehn's achievement; his programme had included the arduous *Hammerklavier* Piano Sonata. Of Hoehn's performance he says:

> 'He played this great work magnificently, as a mature master. This music was in him — it sounded as spontaneous as if he had just composed it. I was deeply impressed by the noble conception of the first movement and moved by

the simply and beautifully played *Adagio*. The
final difficult fugue was splendid; the whole
Sonata was a masterly performance.'

Two days after the competition, Rubinstein and Hoehn performed together, each including the *Hammerklavier* Sonata in his programme. The critics found Rubinstein's interpretation too romantic and that of Hoehn too correct and less exciting. In conversation with his friend, André Diederichs, Rubinstein later declared: 'The truth is we were both right.'

When asked to defend this apparent contradiction, Rubinstein replied:

'[If] you ask ten famous artists to paint you, your
face will be *different* on each picture but the
painters will assure you they *interpreted* your face
exactly as they see.'

Elaborating his views, he added:

'[Each] creative work becomes a part of the
universe, just like a flower, or human being.
Consequently, a sonata sounds *different* to each
gifted interpreter. This is the real mission of our
particular talents.'

Arthur Rubinstein, *My Young Years, London*: Jonathan Cape, 1973, p. 339 and p. 355.

Rubinstein recalled his time in Paris during the Great War. He visited a hospital where soldiers were being treated. He recounts how his eyes caught sight of an upright piano in the corner of the room. It was abominably out of tune and two or three keys were mute but he sat down and began to play:

> 'I played the Sonata *Pathétique* of Beethoven; I had never played it like that before. It was not how it sounded it was how I felt. I was ready to cry, and so was everyone present.'

Arthur Rubinstein, op. cit., 1973, p. 437.

JOHN RUSSELL

The statesman Sir John Russell made a tour of Germany in the years 1820–22 and had occasion to meet with Beethoven and hear him perform at the piano – although by then Beethoven's hearing was much impaired. He has left the following account of Beethoven's efforts to come to terms with his affliction:

> 'The moment he is seated at the piano he is evidently unconscious that there is anything else in existence ... The muscles of his face swell and its veins stand out; the wild eye rolls doubly wild; the mouth quivers; and Beethoven looks like a wizard overpowered by the demons he has called up ... And considering how very deaf he is, it seems impossible that he should hear all he plays. Accordingly, when playing softly, he does not bring out a single note. He hears it in his "mind's ear", while his eye, and the almost imperceptible motion of his fingers, shows that he is following out the strain in his own soul through all its dying gradations.'

Sir John Russell cited in: Oscar George Theodore Sonneck,

Beethoven: Impressions of contemporaries, London: Oxford University Press, 1927, p. 115. Russell's reminiscences are also quoted in, Harold C. Schonberg, *The Great Pianists,* London: Victor Gollancz, 1964, p. 88.

MATTHEW RYE

The British musicologist Matthew Rye affirms Beethoven's contention that he never repeated himself:

> 'No two of Beethoven's 32 piano sonatas are alike. Even more than his string quartets, which similarly span his creative life, he seemed to make new strides in form and motivic development in each work. Yet the last five sonatas stand apart from the rest, in the same way that the late quartets do from their predecessors. Opp. 101, 106, 109, 110 and 111 enter new levels of scale and ambition — and all were intended to be published with the designation "for the *Hammerklavier*", the German equivalent of the "Pianoforte", though only Op. 106 appeared in print with this instruction.'

Matthew Rye, *Notes to the BBC Radio Three Beethoven Experience,* Friday 10 June 2005, www.bbc.co.uk/radio3/Beethoven

CAMILLE SAINT-SAËNS

The French composer, organist, conductor and pianist Camille Saint-Saëns was one of the most remarkable musical child prodigies in history. At the age of five he performed to private audiences and when age ten made his public debut in Paris at the Salle Pleyel. His programme included

Mozart's Piano Concerto in B flat, K450 and Beethoven's Third Piano Concerto. Most remarkably, Saint-Saëns played from memory. At the close of the concert he offered to give as an encore any of the Beethoven Piano sonatas. At over the age of sixty he repeated the offer at a concert to the musical elect of Madrid. Towards the end of his long life (86), Saint-Saëns maintained diligent morning practice by performing scales and arpeggios — relieving what he considered to be the tedium by simultaneously reading the morning newspaper that he placed on the piano's music rack!

Adapted, in part, from James Harding, *Saint-Saëns and his Circle*, London: Chapman & Hall, 1965, p. 18.

Saint-Saëns paid homage to Beethoven in his *Variations on a Theme by Beethoven*, Op. 35. These take the form of a duo composed for four hands on two pianos. The main theme is taken from Beethoven's Sonata in E flat, Op. 31, No. 3. Saint-Saëns' ten variations are lively and technically demanding. Throughout the piece the two pianos trade-off between playing and waiting in a manner that is exciting to observe in performance. The two protagonists exchange rapidly alternating chords that are shared between the two pianos, much as they alternate between the lower and upper registers of the keyboard in Beethoven's original *Menuetto*.

An amusing anecdote recalls the occasion when Saint-Saëns himself took part in a performance of his *Variations*, and, quite uncharacteristically, lost his nerve in the 'diabolical finale'.

> '[He] rushed headlong at the *Presto* — with his partner gallantly following — and won the breathless race with only a bar's difference between them.'

As recounted by James Harding, *Saint-Saëns and his Circle*, London: Chapman & Hall, 1965, pp. 129–30.

Saint-Saëns Variations Op. 35 were dedicated to Alfred and Marie Jaell who performed the work on 28 March 1874 at the Salle Érard in Paris. It was unpublished at the time. Alfred Jaell, a pupil of Saint-Saëns, was, like his teacher, a child prodigy described by the *Revue et Gazette* as possessing artistry having 'miraculous qualities'.

ANTON FELIX SCHINDLER

Anton Felix Schindler was an associate of Beethoven and acted as his secretary, assistant and spokesman in the latter period of the composer's life. He was by training a lawyer although his vocation was in music; he was appointed leader of the violins in the Josephstadt-theatre. Schindler's claim to fame is his early study *Biographie von Ludwig van Beethoven* that was published in Münster in 1840 and again in 1860 in two volumes with extensive revisions and additions. English-speaking readers know this work as *Beethoven as I Knew Him*, edited with commentaries and emendations by Donald W. MacArdle in a translation by Constance S. Jolly, London: Faber and Faber, 1966.

Throughout the nineteenth century, and well into the twentieth, Schindler's *Life* had a considerable influence on the perception of Beethoven and Beethoven biography. Unfortunately for posterity, Schindler destroyed many of the composer's Conversation Books – and possibly other Beethoven memorabilia. In addition, his reliability as a credible chronicler of Beethoven has been called into question. It is now considered he may have inserted spurious entries into a number of the composer's surviving Conversation Books and that his accounts of alleged conversations with the composer, notably about the nature of his music, may have been exaggerated or even invented.

See: Peter Stadlen, *Schindler's Beethoven Forgeries*, *The Musical Times*, Vol. 118, No. 1613, July 1977, pp. 549–552.

Notwithstanding Schindler's indiscretions, as the editor to the 1960 edition of Schindler's text remarks,

> 'The Beethoven who steps forth from these pages is indeed the Beethoven of the *Eroica* and last Quartets ... [and] will give much that cannot be found elsewhere.'

It is from Schindler we learn how Beethoven became interested in the writings of the contemporary mystical poet and musician Christian Schubart. He characterised the musical keys with feelings and ascribed to them a certain 'psyche'.

Schindler, pp. 366–7.

Of the piano sonatas, Schindler enthuses.

> 'The [piano] sonatas alone claim the position of true poetry; they alone are portraits of the heart in the truest meaning of the expression, and therefore are confined within a narrower framework than any other medium performed in public. With the sonata the lover of musical poetry separates himself from all external influences or intrusions upon his feelings, and finds himself alone with his most intimate friend or beloved. Should the work fall false upon his outer ear, the heart will hear it otherwise, for his fantasy, awakened by the tones and harmonies, will correct any technical defects. The sonata is best

> able to inspire reverence in the soul, and often
> lifts it to prayer.'

Schindler, p. 403.

Typical of Schindler's effusive style and the manner of endorsement of his master's work is the following passage:

> 'Consider the form of the first movement of the first Sonata in F minor, how different it is from the form of the first movement of the Sonata in E-flat major, Op. 7! And how different again are the first movements of the Sonata in C minor Op. 10 and the *Pathétique* Op. 13, and so on through the wonderfully inspired Sonatas Op. 57 (F minor), Op. 90 (E minor), right up to the last! Each one different, and yet the master leads us by way of his form along such a sure, clear path that requires little imagination, provided the performance is adapted to the content, to retain the thread of poetry without losing it for even at instant!'

Schindler, p. 405.

Concerning the mood prevailing in the two Piano Sonatas Op. 14, Schindler gives an account of a conversation with Beethoven that he states took place sometime in 1823. He describes how he raised the question with the composer of the 'inner meaning' of his piano sonatas – a subject upon which the composer is known to have been particularly reticent. Regarding the Op. 14 Sonatas, Schindler alleges Beethoven said they embodied a form of dialogue between two principles whose meaning was inherent within the music and which required no interpretive words to be written above the score.

Schindler, p. 406.

In our desire for a better understanding of Beethoven, we want to believe in the veracity of such remarks as the forgoing. On this occasion it has to be conceded some commentators have reservations the conversation ever took place, or, if it did, that Schindler may have elaborated the account to suit his own ends. Harold Truscott is one authority who considers Schindler's remarks to be somewhat fanciful, given Beethoven's reluctance to give detailed interpretations of his compositions.

See: Harold Truscott *The Piano Music* [of Beethoven], in: Denis Arnold and Nigel Fortune, editors, London: Faber and Faber, 1973, p. 102.

Konrad Wolff gives Schindler the benefit of the doubt on this occasion. He discusses Schindler's interpretation of the Op. 14 at some length and considers his views may have some 'inner truth'. He cites the manner in which, from the start,

> 'right hand and left hand are brought into rhythmic and melodic opposition – "pleading" and "resisting".'

See: Konrad Wolff, *Masters of the Keyboard: Individual style elements in the piano music of Bach, Haydn, Mozart, Beethoven, Schubert, Chopin, and Brahms*, Bloomington: Indiana University Press, 1990, p. 157.

William Newman also remarks on the 'personified conflict', thought by some to be inherent within the Op. 14 Piano Sonatas. He then observes, in more everyday terms, how much they differ from their dramatic predecessor the Sonata

Pathétique: '[They] are relatively quiet and intimate, distinguished by their charm, wit, and craftsmanship.'

William Newman, *The Sonata in the Classic Era*, Chapel Hill: University of North Carolina Press 1963, p. 515.

The D minor Piano Sonata, Op. 31, No. 2 bears the designation *The Tempest – Der Sturm* in Beethoven's native language. The origins of this sobriquet may be traced to an anecdote recalled by Schindler. According to his account, he told the composer what a great impression this piece had made upon him when he heard it played by the composer's pupil Carl Czerny (see above). When asked to reveal the meaning inherent in the composition, Schindler states Beethoven gave the laconic reply: 'Just read Shakespeare's *Tempest*.' He was no more explicit.

Schindler p. 406.

The reader will recall Shakespeare's play opens in the midst of a violent storm that rages about an enchanted isle, and contains such memorable lines as: 'The isle is full of noises, sounds and sweet airs.'

Little wonder then, with such implicit musical associations, belief in Schindler's claims seized the imagination of later writers and artists. For example, the German scholar and musicologist Arnold Schering constructed an entire book that purported to establish relationships between Beethoven's piano music and Shakespeare's text.

See: Paul Henry Lang, *Musicology and Performance*, New Haven: Yale University Press, 1997, pp. 238–9.

In response to these romantic imaginings, the German illustrator Alois Kolb depicted Beethoven as a robed figure – probably *The Tempest's* principal character Prospero – standing before tempestuous winds within which hapless maidens are tossed about.

A reproduction of Kolb's illustration can be viewed on the Beethoven House Digital Archives, Library Document

Ley, Band VIII, No. 112.

It is now considered Schindler's anecdote is apocryphal.

See, for example: Barry Cooper, *Beethoven and the Creative Process*, Oxford: Clarendon Press, 1990, p. 42.

Wilfrid Mellers offers a carefully balanced judgement here. He reminds us how, throughout the nineteenth century — a period, let us remember, when Beethoven was being deified — a dominant strand in the estimation of his work 'was founded on the belief his music could best be elucidated by colourful poetic imagery'.

Not surprisingly, such an outlook has nurtured the adoption of sobriquets, such as *The Tempest*, and has served as cues for 'elaborate extra-musical programmes'.

As Mellers points out, even those

> 'predisposed to acknowledging a poetic dimension in music criticism have mistrusted their usefulness, viewing them as either too general, or as only selectively appropriate'.

Wilfrid Howard Mellers, *The Sonata Principle* (from c. 1750), London: Rockliff, 1957, p. 44.

We close our selection of Schindler's writings, by recalling the circumstances that have led to the two movements of the Op. 90 Piano Sonata being characterised, respectively, as a contest between the head and the heart (first movement) and a form of dialogue with a loved one (second movement).

Beethoven dedicated the composition to his friend Count Moritz Lichnowsky. He had a relationship with a singer-actress by the name of Josepha (Johanna) Stummer; she is frequently, and mistakenly, described as being a dancer. Johanna was not of noble birth but must have been a singer of some accomplishments; for example, she sang the role of Donna Elvira in Mozart's *Don Giovanni* and was a member of the Gesellschaft der Musikfreunde. Schindler claims Beethoven had set the Count's love-story to music and that the two movements could be described as: 'Conflict between head and heart' (Moritz wrestling with his uncertainty) and 'Conversations with the Beloved' (Moritz and Johanna united in their mutual affections).

Schindler p. 210.

Thereby Schindler set in motion a body of programmatic interpretation, bearing on the alleged inner meaning of the E minor Piano Sonata, that endured throughout the nineteenth century and beyond.

ARTUR SCHNABEL

In his music-making, the Austrian pianist Artur Schnabel is remembered for his high-mindedness and intellectual seriousness. His interpretations, particularly of the works of Beethoven and Schubert, have been described as 'displaying marked vitality, profundity and spirituality'.

He was the first pianist to record the complete cycle of the 32 piano sonatas of Beethoven that he accomplished between 1932 and 1935 on the British HMV label. This achievement prompted the musicologist Harold C. Schonberg to dub Schnabel as 'the man who invented Beethoven'.

Harold C. Schonberg, *The Great Pianists*, London: Victor Gollancz, 1964.

Schnabel's first performance of the Beethoven piano-sonata cycle was in 1927 for an organisation called *The People's Stage*. The architect Oskar Kaufmmann designed their auditorium — he also designed the title pages for some of Schnabel's own early compositions. Reflecting on his performance of the Beethoven piano sonatas Schnabel recalls:

'I played the complete cycle of the thirty-two Beethoven sonatas (each time in recitals) only four times in my life: twice in Berlin, once in London and once in New York. In Berlin I repeated the cycle, this time at the *Philharmonie*, the hall where all the orchestral concerts of the Berlin Philharmonic Orchestra took place, during the winter season of 1932–3.'

In the meantime, the National Socialists came to power. Of this Schnabel recalls:

'The right to broadcast my seven concerts — the cycle of the thirty-two Beethoven sonatas — had been bought by the state-controlled German Broadcasting Company. Apparently, when Hitler took over they were commanded to stop broadcasting these concerts, for the last three recitals of my series, from February on, were not broadcast. I found out about this only from the people who wanted to hear my concerts on the radio (the hall was a sell out) because the Broadcasting Company never notified me.'

In 1945, with the ending of the war, Schnabel gave an address at the University of Chicago. At its conclusion, he took questions from the audience. One student asked if the difference between Beethoven's pianos and those of today should be considered in performance. Schnabel replied:

'It should. But the result will not be to disavow Beethoven's very daring and revealing use of

> the pedal. I have had access to the marvellous collections in Vienna and in Berlin. I have played Bach's, Beethoven's, Weber's and other pianos. In Beethoven's case the effect of the pedalizations demanded by him was exactly the same on the old instruments as on the new ones. In all his compositions for piano Beethoven made only thirty or a few more pedal marks ... The markings by Beethoven have to be observed under all circumstances, in every room or mood or company, because they are an inseparable part of the music as such, and if one does not observe these pedal marks, the music is changed.'

Artur Schnabel, *My Life and Music*, London: Longmans, 1961, p. 105 et seq.

Schnabel is also remembered for his performing edition of the Beethoven sonatas. Commenting on this, the pianist Leon Fleisher remarked:

> 'His edition of the Beethoven sonatas is so instructive because his ideas and suggestions are in a different print than what Beethoven wrote; you can always distinguish between Beethoven and Schnabel. But that kind of dedication, that kind of musical integrity to the desires and instructions from the composer, gave it an authenticity that was irresistible, and that was combined with his level of inspiration.'

Leon Fleisher in interview with Elijah Ho, October 1, 2014.

*

In his 1945 interview with the music students at the University of Chicago, one student remarked:

> 'You have edited many of the compositions of Beethoven. How do you go about editing the music of a man who is dead?'

Schnabel replied:

> 'I edited Beethoven's thirty-two sonatas in the twenties. Maybe I would proceed differently now. When I first tried my hand at editing, in 1912, I was not yet as conscientious, and much less experienced than in the twenties. For the Beethoven edition which, as a whole, I think to be still usable, I tried to get hold of as much original material as possible — manuscripts, first and second editions of which Beethoven had seen the proofs. In the case of different versions in manuscripts and in the printed editions which Beethoven had seen the proofs, I decided on the printed version, because Beethoven was not always too careful in his manuscripts, knowing that he would see the proofs ... The metronome markings — with the one exception of Opus 106 where Beethoven has provided them — are my choice and responsibility, but are never intended to be more than suggestions.'

Artur Schnabel, *My Life and Music*, London: Longmans, 1961, pp. 130–1.

Schnabel's playing has not always found favour. In March 1944, he gave an all-Beethoven recital in the Carnegie Hall comprising: the Piano Sonatas Opp. 10, No. 2; 31, No. 2; 110; and 111. The reviewer (unnamed but probably Virgil Thomson — see below) felt disposed to remark:

> 'Artur Schnabel, who played last night in the Carnegie Hall the second of three recitals ... devoted to the piano music of Beethoven, has for some thirty or forty years made this composer the object of his special attention. He passes, indeed, and with reason, for an expert on the subject ... His ideas about Beethoven's piano music in general, whether or not one finds his readings convincing, are not to be dismissed lightly. Neither need they, I think, be taken as the voice of authority. For all the consistency and logic of his musicianship, there is too large a modicum of late-nineteenth-century Romanticism in Mr. Schnabel's own personality to make his Beethoven — who was, after all, a child of the late eighteenth — wholly convincing to musicians of the mid-twentieth. No one wants to deny the Romantic elements in Beethoven, but I do think that they are another kind of Romanism from Schnabel's, which seems to be based on the Wagnerian theories of expressivity.'

Cited in: Virgil Thomson, *The Musical Scene*, New York: Greenwood Press, 1968, p.192.

Arthur Rubinstein was not always impressed by Schnabel's playing. He is on record as remaking:

> 'I was never convinced by the intellectual and almost pedantic conception of Artur Schnabel,

the acknowledged specialist in these works. He sounded to me as if he were giving lessons to us in the audience.'

Arthur Rubinstein, *My Many Years*, London: Jonathan Cape, 1980, p. 159.

Schnabel was one of the few artists to perform the *Hammerklavier* Sonata at Beethoven's original tempo indications. Writing of his performance, Martin Cooper states:

'Artur Schnabel decided to take Beethoven at his word and to play the first movement of Op. 106 at the tempo so long considered impossible. He did not wholly convince listeners by his own performance in which the fullness of the fast chordal passages and the wealth of detail in inner parts were not ideally clear, and his example has not been generally followed by subsequent performers, even those with larger hands and greater facility than Schnabel's.'

A less generous commentator than Cooper condemned Schnabel's adherence to Beethoven's stipulations as an act of 'mistaken piety'.

Martin Cooper, *Beethoven: The last decade, 1817-1827*, London: Oxford University Press, 1970, p. 159.

It is now universally acknowledged — with the possible exception of Artur Schnabel — that Beethoven's tempo indications to the Piano Sonata Op. 106 are unrealistically too fast. In the words of Alfred Brendel:

'The metronome marks ... with one exception ... are all hurried, not to say mechanically over-

> driven. In the first movement particularly, the prescribed tempo cannot be attained, or even approached, on any instrument in the world, by any player at all, be he the devil incarnate, with grievous loss of dynamics, colour and clarity.'

Alfred Brendel, *Alfred Brendel on Music: Collected essays*, Chicago, Iliinois: A Cappella Books, 2001, p. 33.

An anecdote connects us with Artur Schnabel once more and the last of Beethoven's piano sonatas. In his recollections he relates:

> 'A friend of mine in Frankfurt-am-Main was the famous Louis Koch. I mention him because he had one of the finest collections of musical and other precious manuscripts. Each time I went to Frankfurt he invited me to spend hours in his house alone. His housekeeper had instructions to open to me whatever I was interested in. So in that house, quite by myself, I read or played from manuscript works like some of the last Beethoven Sonatas and the last three Schubert sonatas. It was an inestimable experience.'

Artur Schnabel, 1961, p. 63.

Schnabel is known for his sense of humour. While on a tour of Spain, he wrote to his wife saying that during a performance of Beethoven's *Diabelli* Variations he had begun to feel sorry for the audience: 'I am the only person here who is enjoying this, and I get the money; they pay and have to suffer.'

On another occasion he remarked:

> 'The notes I handle no better than many pianists.
> But the pauses between the notes — ah, that is
> where the art resides.'

Comparing composers he once stated: 'Mozart is a garden, Schubert is a forest in light and shade, but Beethoven is a mountain range.'

There were times when even Schnabel's sense of humour and equanimity must have been severely tested, as, for example, on an occasion when he was performing Beethoven's Piano Sonata Op. 101. The circumstance in question relates to a period, just before the outbreak of the Great War, when Schnabel was on a concert tour of what was then East Prussia. We let him take up the tale:

> 'I remember one place where I played Beethoven's Sonata Op. 101 as the first item. As you know it opens with a very delicate movement. The retired sergeant, who had been selling programmes and tickets at a table behind the last row, counted his takings during this delicate movement, throwing copper and sliver coins onto a china plate which he had ready on his table.'

The clatter of the coins proved too much, even for the equably disposed Schnabel; he had to request the sergeant to stop counting and to start all over again. He magnanimously reflected that the sergeant was only doing his job and no one had forewarned him.

Artur Schnabel, 1961, pp. 48–9.

The American composer and music critic Virgil Thomson heard Artur Schnabel perform on March 28 1944. His programme included the Piano Sonata Op. 110. By then

Thomson had earned a reputation for his wit, candour and independent-minded judgement in his capacity of music critic for the *New York Herald-Tribune*. Notwithstanding that by then Schnabel had also earned a reputation for his interpretations of the piano works of Beethoven, and, we may add, for the 'rediscovery' from years of neglect of the piano sonatas of Franz Schubert, Thomson was clearly not in awe of Schnabel's performance. In his review of the concert, Thomson reflected on Schnabel's many years of study of Beethoven and of his standing as an artist of distinction:

> 'He passes, indeed, and with reason, for an expert on the subject, by which is usually meant that his knowledge of it is extensive and that his judgements about it are respected ... His readings about Beethoven's piano music in general, whether or not one finds his readings convincing, are not to be dismissed lightly.'

We should add here, by way of amplification of Thomson's remarks, that in 1932 Schnabel had completed the first recoding ever of Beethoven's complete set of piano sonatas and at about the same time had published the meticulously thorough performing edition of these works to which we have made mention.

Of Schnabel's interpretation, Thomson considered the master unduly emphasized what Thomson regarded as the composition's 'secondary material':

Mr. Schnabel does not admit, or plays as if he did not admit, any difference between the expressive functions of melody and passage work. The neutral material of music — scales, arpeggiated basses, accompanying figures, ostinato chordal backgrounds, formal cadences — he plays as if they were as intense communication, as if they were saying something as important as the main thematic material. They are important to Beethoven's composition, of course; but they are not directly expressive musical elements. They serve as amplification, as underpinning, frequently as mere acoustical brilliance. To execute them all with climactic emphasis is to rob the melodic material, the expressive phrases, of their singing power.'

Virgil Thomson, *The Musical Scene*, New York: Greenwood Press, 1968, pp. 192–3.

ARNOLD SCHOENBERG

In a letter to Ferruccio Busoni, the Austrian composer and music theorist Arnold Schoenberg remarked about some recently composed piano pieces of his own, adding:

> 'There can be no doubt that the piano-style of a period bears a certain resemblance to its orchestral style. I find that one can even see this in Mozart and Beethoven. All those for whom expression was the principal concern *composed for the piano* in that they *composed* according to the instrument's needs and demands. Composition is the dominant factor; one takes the instrument into account. Not the contrary.'

Antony Beaumont, editor, *Ferruccio Busoni: Selected letters*, London: Faber and Faber, 1987, pp. 135–6 and p. 387.

HAROLD CHARLES SCHONBERG

In his survey *The Great Pianists*, the American music critic and journalist Harold Charles Schonberg considers

Beethoven as the first romantic pianist:

> 'In many things Beethoven was ahead of his time, and so was his piano playing. It had unprecedented power, personality and emotional appeal. In many respects he can be considered the first romantic pianist: the one who broke all the laws in the name of expression (for in the nineteenth century the word "expression" was to take the place of the eighteenth-century "taste"); the one who thought orchestrally and achieved orchestral effects on the piano. In that, he was alone in his day and his like was not to be seen until the maturity of Liszt.'

In this context he further remarks:

> 'Why ... is Beethoven's own piano music so relatively conservative, not to say often old-fashioned, in its layout? Clementi, Dussek, even Steibelt added more to piano technique on the printed page than almost anything to be found in the Beethoven sonatas, incomparably greater musically as the latter are. One answer would be, of course, that with Beethoven the idea counted more than its execution. His sonatas are not necessarily conceived in terms of the piano *per se*, but in terms of ideas expressed in form. Some of the piano writing can be frightfully difficult, but it is not "pianistic." There is a great difference.'

Harold C. Schonberg, *The Great Pianists*, London: Victor Gollancz, 1996, p. 74 and p. 272.

*

CLARA SCHUMANN

Born Clara Josephine Wieck, Clara Schuman was considered to be one of the most distinguished pianists of the Romantic era. For more than sixty years she appeared before the public in recitals that did much to promote a greater awareness of Beethoven's piano sonatas. From December 1837 to April 1838, she performed a series of recitals in Vienna when she was still only 18. One of these included the challenging *Appassionata*, Op. 57. Her interpretation prompted Franz Grillparzer, Austria's leading dramatic poet, to write a poem in her honour entitled 'Clara Wieck and Beethoven'.

Following her marriage to the composer Robert Schuman, Clara, herself an accomplished composer, kept a marriage diary. An entry for July 1842 bears testimony to her determination to progress with her pianistic attainments through her application to the works of Bach and Beethoven:

> 'This week I have started to play regularly at least 2 hours a day. I play mostly fugues [of Bach] and sonatas by Beethoven, but soon I also want to return in earnest once more to Robert's compositions.'

In response, Robert remarked:

> 'Clara has been working diligently on several Beethoven sonatas and conceives of them in quite a unique way without compromising the original. That gives me great satisfaction.'

Gerd Nauhaus, editor, *The Marriage Diaries of Robert & Clara Schumann*, London: Robson Books, 1994, pp. 98–9.

*

A further recollection from the past connects us to an evening when two great artists were brought together in a performance of the Piano Sonata Op. 57. The evening in question was sometime in 1874 when several friends had been invited to hear Mendelssohn perform — one of them being Clara Schumann. At one point in his rectal, Mendelssohn played the F minor Piano Sonata. At the end of the *Andante* he deliberately held the final chord for a long time, by way of securing the attention of the audience. At this he rose, and turning to Clara said: 'You must play the Finale.'

The composer-pianist Ferdinand Hiller, a close friend of Mendelssohn, was among the invited guests, and records how at first Clara 'strongly protested' but finally yielded to Mendelssohn's entreaties and performed the Finale. In Hiller's estimation:

> 'The end was worthy of the beginning, and if the order had been reversed it would no doubt have been just as fine.'

Ferdinand Hiller, *Mendelssohn: Letters and recollections*, New York: Vienna House, 1972, p. 167.

Clara performed the *Les Adieux* Piano Sonata at a recital she gave in Vienna in February 1856. A measure of her formidable stamina is that she also included in her programme the *Hammerklavier* Sonata. Worthy of mention is that by this time she was the mother of seven children and in addition, with the declining health of her celebrated husband, had to increasingly provide for the needs of the family. Notwithstanding her status as one of the most celebrated interpreters of her age — some would say second only to Franz Liszt — her detractors felt she was too inclined, on occasion, to exhibit virtuosity at the expense of musical feeling and expression. For example, following the recital just mentioned the contributor to the March issue of the *Berlinische Monatschrift für Theater und Kunst* complained of 'her untrammelled love of the fastest tempo'.

As recalled by Anton Felix Schindler in: *Beethoven as I Knew Him*, edited by Donald W. MacArdle and translated by Constance S. Jolly from the German edition of 1860, London: Faber and Faber 1966, pp. 434–5.)

Schindler also held similar opinions of Clara's playing.

Perhaps Clara's style of interpretation had mellowed towards the end of her career as a concert pianist, since the musicologist John Fuller-Maitland felt disposed to give the following generous account of her playing:

> 'Never can I forget Clara Schumann's eloquent interpretation of the Sonata [Op. 81a] on one of her last appearances in London. The poignancy of the first movement, the loneliness of the section labelled "Absence", and the rapture of the meeting in the last movement, were so movingly given that one could not help imagining a personal application, although I cannot now believe that the great artist was conscious of it at the time.'

Fuller-Maitland then suggests the audience itself was emotionally carried away by Clara's playing:

> 'It was inevitable at that stage of English musical culture, that there should be a round of applause after what seemed to be the three final chords near the end, and the player's quiet

> resumption of the theme must have conveyed a
> severe reproof to some of her too enthusiastic
> admirers.'

John Fuller-Maitland, *Special Issue* [Death Centenary], *Musical Times*, London, Vol. VIII, No. 2, 1927, p. 221.

ALEXANDER SCRIABIN

The Russian composer and pianist Alexander Scriabin is recognized for his contribution to the development of the atonal system, independently of Arnold Schoenberg, and of his disposition to mysticism. In recent times, his system of musical aesthetics has been reevaluated and some consider the invention enshrined within his ten published sonatas for piano, provide one of the most consistent contribution to the genre since those of Beethoven. Margarita Morozova was an accomplished pupil of Alexander Scriabin and Nikolai Medtner, at the Leningrad Conservatoire. The following is an extract from her recollections of her two teachers:

> 'When Scriabin played Beethoven he couldn't
> help colouring him with his own bright individu-
> ality ... Medtner, on the other hand, would put
> himself in the background. What emerged was
> not Medtner but Beethoven.'

Scriabin, Morozova recalls, was given to making impassioned exhortations to his piano pupils:

> 'No dry passages! Everything must live! Smear
> the difficult bits if you must, but if they end
> brilliantly, then you'll still have the impression of
> cleanness and splendour! Play it all ... in one

breath! The thrill ... before all else! The atmosphere of art above all else! ... You must draw sound from wood and steel as a miner extracts precious ore from the earth. Don't play like you're washing laundry.'

Faubio Bowers, *Scriabin: A biography*, Mineola: Dover; London: Constable, 1996, pp. 288–9.

PETER SERKIN

The American pianist Peter Serkin considers the revolutionary in Beethoven:

'His music was revolutionary, and it retains that characteristic as far as I'm concerned. And as interpreters, we need to rediscover this. This doesn't mean we have to invent contrived, quirky ways of playing his music. We don't have to inject the music with a bold revolutionary character; we just have to find it.'

Peter Serkin in, David Dubal, *The World of the Concert Pianist*, London: Victor Gollancz, 1998, pp. 299–300.

JOHN SHEDLOCK

John Shedlock was a nineteenth-century English pianist, musicologist and music critic. He lectured at the Royal Academy of Music and contributed to the London *Musical Times*. He wrote an account of a copy of Cramer's Studies, with notes by Beethoven, which he discovered in Berlin in 1893. He is remembered today for his study of Beethoven's piano sonatas.

Shedlock is one of many writers to cite what is perhaps the most frequently quoted aphorism in the whole of Beethoven piano-literature:

> 'Bach's forty-eight Preludes and Fugues and Beethoven's thirty-two Sonatas tower above all other works written for the pianoforte; they were aptly described by the late Dr. Hans von Bülow, the one as the *Old Testament*, the other as the *New Testament* of musical literature. Each fresh study of them reveals new points of interest, new beauties; they are rich mines which it is impossible to exhaust.'

Elsewhere Shedlock adds:

> 'The great sonatas of Beethoven are not mere cunningly devised pieces, not mere mood-painting; they are real, living dramas. In aiming at a higher organisation, he actually became a disorganiser. "All things are growing or decaying", says Herbert Spencer. And in Beethoven, so far as sonata and sonata form are concerned, we seem, as it were, to perceive the beginning of a period of decay.'

John South Shedlock, *Beethoven's Pianoforte Sonatas: The origin and respective values of various readings*, London: Augener Ltd., 1918, p. 19. See also: John South Shedlock, *The Pianoforte Sonata: Its origin and development*, London: Methuen, 1895, p. 191.

*

JOHN SLOBODA

In his extensive study of the psychology of music, Professor John Sloboda remarks:

> 'Musical performance is an incredibly complex and multi-layered phenomenon. To carry off a Beethoven sonata requires so much that any one psychologist can study only a bit of it at a time. I've been particularly interested in the improvisatory aspect of performance, because even though the notes of a Beethoven sonata are specified, there is a great deal of freedom for the performer to interpret. Indeed, if you just played a piece of classical music as written on the page it would be very dull. A great deal of the art of good performance is the added values you give to the performance, and I've been trying to study whether there is a systematic way in which good performers add that value.'

John Sloboda cited in: Michael Oliver, editor, *Settling the Score: A journey through the music of the twentieth century*, London: Faber and Faber, 1999, p. 229.

See also the following works of Sloboda: *Musical Perceptions*, New York: Oxford University Press, 1994, pp. 290, (with Rita Aiello); *The Origins and Development of Musical Competence*, London: Oxford University Press/Paris: Presses Universitaires de France, 1995, (editor, with Irene Deliege); *Perception and Cognition of Music*, Psychologists' Press, 1997, (editor, with Irene Deliege); *Music and Emotion: Theory and Research*, Oxford: Oxford University Press, 2001, p. 487, (editor, with Patrik N Juslin); and *Exploring the Musical Mind: Cognition: Emotion: Ability: Function*, Oxford: Oxford University Press, 2005.

LEOPOLD STOKOWSKI

David Raskin, the composer and orchestrator of many Hollywood film classics, collaborated with Leopold Stokowski and has left this account:

> 'If anybody thinks that Stokowski didn't orchestrate his own music, I am here to refute that ... The first assignment *Stoki* gave me was a Beethoven piano sonata. It was all marked up in his handwriting for instrumentation, and he asked me to orchestrate according to those directions. The marking was so meticulous, that a second-year harmony student could have done it just as he wanted it.'

Abram Chasins, *Leopold Stokowski, A profile*, New York: Hawthorn Books, 1979, p. 266.

IGOR STRAVINSKY

In his *Autobiography*, Igor Stravinsky pays homage to Beethoven's piano music:

> 'I recognized in him [Beethoven] the indisputable monarch of the instrument. It is the instrument that inspires his thought and determines its substance. The relations of a composer to his sound-medium may be of two kinds. Some, for example, compose music *for* the piano; others compose *piano music.* Beethoven is clearly in the second category. In all his immense pianistic work, it is the "instrumental" side which is characteristic of him and makes him infinitely precious to me. It is the giant instrumentalist that

predominates in him, and it is thanks to that quality that he cannot fail to reach any ear that is open to music.'

Igor Stravinsky, *An Autobiography*, London: Calder and Boyars, 1975, p. 116.

From his review of the works of various writers commentating on Beethoven's piano sonatas, Stravinsky remarks:

'It remains to be said that [Eric] Blom is a more resourceful guide in the early sonatas than in the late ones, but that this is a lesser disadvantage than the other way round, as the majority of the sonatas *are* early; more than half of them antedate the Second Symphony, in fact, and more than two thirds are pre-*Eroica*. And Blom's presentation of these earlier works is at the same time simple and comprehensive, including, as it does, a survey of the elements of the form as Beethoven inherited it — of the principle of thematic duality, for instance ... And, finally, Blom succeeds in his aim, which is to help the reader follow the growth of the form in Beethoven and to enable him to appreciate Beethoven's enlargements.'

Igor Stravinsky, 'On Beethoven's Piano Sonatas'*,* in*: Themes and Conclusions*, London: Faber and Faber, 1972, p, 268.

In his discussion of the Piano Sonata Op. 106, Stravinsky remarked: 'Much of the first movement could be included in my category of orchestral sonata.' He considered the third movement to be

> 'the richest harmonically of all [Beethoven's] sonatas, in so far as that element can be thought of separately'.

Igor Stravinsky, 1972, p. 272.

Writing of Beethoven's final trilogy of piano sonatas, Stravinsky comments:

> 'The three final Sonatas represent a great ventilation in style — what a more Augustan writer would describe as a rediscovery of the classical spirit ... Beethoven's path of discovery tended, at the end, to lead more and more to contrapuntal means, homophonic thematic developments giving way to thematic transformation in variation and fugue.'

Igor Stravinsky, 1972, pp. 272–3.

PETER TCHAIKOVSKY

Nadezhda von Meck, Tchaikovsky's patroness and confidante from 1877 to 1890, wrote to her protégée in 1878 with her views concerning the programmatic nature she considered to be evident in certain of Beethoven's piano sonatas — unspecified. Her letter prompted the following responses from Tchaikovsky:

> 'In my opinion, any music is programme music. There's no other kind because, for example, symphonies have a programme, overtures even more so, and operas definitely. I know Beethoven sonatas, one of which represents the movement of a wheel [Tchaikovsky is probably thinking here

of the *Les Adieux* Piano Sonata, Op. 81a with its associations of a coach taking leave of Beethoven's patron the Archduke Rudolph.] and another a quarrel between husband and wife [Tchaikovsky is probably thinking here of the Piano Sonata, Op. 90 with its alleged associations between Count Moritz Lichnowsky and Josepha (Johanna) Stummer.] ... Programme music was invented by *Beethoven*, to some extent in the *Eroica* Symphony, but more particularly in the Sixth, the *Pastoral* ... I think Beethoven was wrong not to give a programme for the sonatas you mention. In any case, as I see it, both kinds of music (instrumental and orchestral) have an equal raison d'être, and I don't understand those gentlemen who recognize only one category to the exclusion of the other.'

Edward Garden and Nigel Gottrei, editors, '*To My best Friend*': *Correspondence between Tchaikovsky and Nadezhda von Meck, 1876–1878*, Oxford: Clarendon Press, 1993.

ALEXANDER WHEELOCK THAYER

The American-born scholar, historian and musicologist Alexander Wheelock Thayer is Beethoven's most respected pioneering biographer. His lifetime study of the composer elevated Beethoven scholarship to an entirely new level of authority. It was during his graduate years at Harvard University that Thayer developed his interest in Beethoven musicology. He was disposed in this direction in part by discrepancies he found in Anton Schindler's writings (see above) and what to him appeared to be the more objective accounts in the recollections of others who had known Beethoven. In particular, the recollections of Beethoven's former piano pupil Ferdinand Ries and those of the composer's close friend Franz Gerhard Wegeler stirred Thayer. Together, in 1838, they published a pioneering account of the composer under the title *Biographische Notizen über Ludwig van Beethoven*. This was significant for Beethoven scholarship since it included for the first time extracts from the composer's letters written to the authors. As Thayer's editor Elliot Forbes remarks:

> 'The historian in Thayer was awakened, and he determined to bring Schindler's biography and the *Notizen* of Wegeler and Ries and other material from English sources [and others] into an ordered account.'

As Thayer progressed with his work he indefatigably derived material from a variety of sources including: court records, contemporary notices and accounts of concerts and recitals, Beethoven's own documents — letters, sketches, memoranda, and Conversation Books — and reminiscences from those still alive who had some connection with Beethoven or who had personal recollection of him. Thayer was concerned primarily with facts about Beethoven, the man and his music. In his own words:

> 'I fight for no theories and cherish no prejudices; my sole point of view is the truth ... I have resisted the temptation to discuss the character of his [Beethoven's] works and to make such a discussion the foundation of historical speculation, preferring to leave such matters to those who have a greater predilection for them.'

The first edition of Thayer's biography was published in German in three volumes, covering Beethoven's life to 1816; these appeared between 1866 and 1879. The work was completed (1907–08) by Thayer's German colleague Herman Deiters and after his death by Hugo Rieman who incorporated Thayer's notes, covering the years 1817 to Beethoven's death in 1827. Henry E. Krehbiel published the first English edition of the biography in 1921. The most recent version of the biography is that revised and edited in a single volume by Elliot Forbes (1964) with further revisions (1967).

Thayer's achievement has won universal praise as has the man himself:

> 'His industry, zeal, keen power of analysis, candor and fair-mindedness won the confidence of all with whom he came into contact except the literary charlatans whose romances he was bent on destroying in the interest of the verities of history.'

Elliot Forbes, editor, *Thayer's Life of Beethoven*, Princeton, New Jersey: Princeton University Press, 1967, pp. I–xviii.

VIRGIL THOMSON

The American composer and music critic Virgil Thomson gave the following advice to a young pianist who had failed in a piano competition for which Thomson had been a judge on January 26 1971:

> '[For] Beethoven I suggest that you "orchestrate" with your fingers while observing an [interpreta-

tion] modeled on that of someone's recording. Someone who appears to you as being authentic, that is to say, traditional without stuffiness.'

He added:

'Busoni and Rachmaninoff had that quality. Rubinstein often does. Clifford Curzon can open up the long works of Schubert and Schuman by giving them a "line". Landowska could do it with Mozart piano sonatas.'

Tim Page and Vanessa Weeks, editors, *Selected Letters of Virgil Thomson*, New York: Summit Books, 1988.

DONALD FRANCIS TOVEY

The name of Professor, Sir Donald Francis Tovey is indubitably associated with that of Beethoven, notwithstanding his wider accomplishments as a composer, pianist, conductor and authority on the preludes and fugues of J. S. Bach. It is no exaggeration to say that his writings on music have influenced a whole generation and continue to be a point of reference. Tovey began to study and compose at an early age, eventually gaining some fame as a composer. He was widely known in musical circles and became a close friend of Johannes Brahms. As Ried Professor of music at the University of Edinburgh he founded the Ried Orchestra for the performances of which he contributed a series of programme notes that he subsequently edited, enlarged and published as *Essays in Musical Analysis*. Perhaps the work for which Tovey is most widely known is his *Beethoven: Sonatas for Pianoforte*, published for the Associated Board of the Royal Schools of Music in collaboration with Harold

Craxton. Originally published in 1931 it has remained in print. It is from this work that we quote the following from the *Introductory Note* by the editors, John B. McEwen, Principal of the Royal College of Music and Hugh P. Allen, Director of the Royal College of Music:

> '*The Pianoforte Sonatas of Beethoven* must always be among the choicest possessions of all who love music and especially of those who make music their main interest and study ... Models of coherence and lucidity, they provide the musician with examples of never tiring self-criticism in the pursuit of ideal perfection. A vivid commentary on the Composer's life, they allow us to see a great and tragic personality both re-acting to circumstances and at the same time controlling circumstances. And, further, the discerning student may see in them how the personal experience of the composer broadens out into a universalised significance that speaks to and evokes response from the heart of humanity ... While the enlightened use of these sonatas carries with it the privilege of being admitted, if we will, into the companionship of a great mind dealing with problems of beauty in music and its presentation, there exists also, in the too great concentration that may be brought to the literal side of performance, the danger of missing the marvellous spirit that lies behind, and in, the music itself.'

Harold Craxton and Donald Francis Tovey, *Beethoven: Sonatas for Pianoforte*, London: The Associated Board, [1931].

*

RICHARD WAGNER

The following is derived from Richard Wagner's extensive prose works:

> '[Beethoven] the métier of pianoforte-players ... which he had to adopt in order "to be something in the profession", brought him into lasting and most familiar contact with the pianoforte-compositions of the masters of the period. In this department the *sonata* had become the model form. We might say that Beethoven was and remained a sonata-composer, for in the great majority and the most eminent of his instrumental works the sonata form was a veil through which he looked into the realm of tones, or — to put it another way — through which he spoke to us from out that realm.'

William Ashton Ellis, *Richard Wagner's Prose Works: Vol. 5, Actors and Singers*, edited and translated by William Ashton Ellis, London: Kegan Paul, Trench, Trübner, 1896, p. 81.

Two particular recollections connect Wagner with Beethoven and his Piano Sonata Op. 106. As we have implied (see entry for Igor Stravinsky), the first movement contains a number of symphonic features. In the words of Michael Broyles:

> 'The opening gesture ... the broad forte theme ... the wide spacing of the closing theme [with its] simple driving rhythm ... The *Hammerklavier* Sonata is symphonic in conception but thoroughly pianistic in gesture.'

Michael Broyles, *Beethoven: The emergence and evolution of Beethoven's heroic style*, New York: Excelsior Music Publishing Co., 1987, p. 226.

An entry from the Diary of Cosima Wagner (4 November 1872) has direct bearing on the foregoing:

> '[Richard] tells me he has been going through the first movement of Beethoven's B-flat Sonata and was quite overwhelmed by the beauty and tenderness and richness of its detail, which passes by in such a way that nobody notices all that has been put into it ... He talks about orchestrating this sonata, in order to make it more accessible.'

At this point Wagner remarked:

> 'As it is, only the greatest of virtuosos can play it, but if it were performed as orchestrated by me, a sort of tradition could be established.'

Cosima concludes:

> 'We read though the sonata together with incredible delight, its richness of detail is like flowers hidden in a meadow.'

Gregor-Dellin and Dietrich Mack, editors, *Cosima Wagner's Diaries, Vol. 1, 1869 – 1877*, London: Collins, 1978-1980, p. 551.

Our second recollection recalls the playing of Franz Liszt, Wagner's father-in-law, and relates to the occasion of the first Bayreuth Festival in 1876. Liszt and some close friends were invited to dine at Wagner's *Wahnfried* Villa. After dinner the conversation turned to Beethoven's late piano sonatas, but Wagner, being tired as a consequence of his involvement with the arrangements for the Festival, left the company. At this juncture Liszt spoke about the *Hammerklavier* Sonata, in particular regarding the *Adagio*. To illustrate his remarks, he went to the piano and played the movement through. Among the distinguished guests was the Hungarian nobleman Count Albert Apponyi. He relates: 'When the last bars of that mysterious work had died away, we stood motionless.'

On hearing Liszt play, Wagner had left his bedroom but respectfully listened in silence until Liszt's playing was concluded. Running down stairs, in his nightshirt, he flung his arms round Liszt's neck and thanked him emotionally in broken phrases, 'for the wonderful gift he had received'.

Derived from Alan Walker, *Franz Liszt. Volume 3, The final years, 1861-1886*, London: Faber and Faber, 1997, note 41, p. 317. See also: Adrian Williams, Oxford: Clarendon Press, 1990, pp. 525–6.

ANTON VON WEBERN

Several of Webern's pupils have left accounts of the composer as their teacher of piano. The following is a selection relating to Beethoven.

Donna Zincover was a gifted girl who came from a wealthy family in Warsaw. She tragically lost her sight in an accident — a circumstance that affected her teacher, Webern, deeply. Notwithstanding her misfortune, she continued her studies of Beethoven's sonatas with Webern. She describes Webern's method of instruction:

'He did not actually teach piano playing, that is, as an instrument with its own technical requirements, but was concerned only with how a particular piece should sound. I would say he taught a Beethoven sonata as he would conduct a symphony. ... Webern could bring out the musical aspects admirably, but he was not exactly interested in technical training. He gave the pupils the right things to play according to their state of technical advancement. He held:

"It does not matter so much what they play but that they play well." ... He thought that sighted and blind people alike must learn to find their way about on a piano mainly by practising, and the will to express oneself musically acts as the stimulus and wellspring for determination and perseverance.'

K. H. Lehrigstein, a junior teaching-colleague of Webern's, recalls Webern's contribution to the 1934–35 Beethoven course at the Israelite Institute for the Blind:

'Webern played the examples from Beethoven's piano sonatas himself. Because his analysis was so detailed, he never had to play as much as the exposition of a single movement. When he came to a technically more difficult bit, he was not perturbed. I remember one instance when he was confronted with a rapid passage leading into something he wanted to show. He simply gave a rough outline of the demanding passage and humorously commented:

' "You know, some people can do it," saying

it with such mock admiration that he made us all laugh.'

Kurt Manschinger studied with Webern for a full six years. He recalls this period in his memoirs:

> 'When analysing a Beethoven sonata or a Brahms symphony, he found so many hidden connections which eluded others, and of which perhaps even the composer themselves might not always have been conscious ... His patience was limitless, and he was very generous with the time allotted to me. A lesson supposed to last one hour usually lasted two. Beethoven, of course, was his god, then came Brahms and Mahler, finally Schoenberg.'

Hans Moldenhauer, *Anton von Webern: A chronicle of his life and work*, London: Victor Gollancz, 1978, p. 288, p. 420 and p. 505.

HUGO WOLF

In his student days, Hugo Wolf applied himself diligently to the study of Beethoven's piano sonatas. Paul Miller recalls:

> 'He spent day after day in the big Vienna library, absorbed in music of every kind, chiefly that of Beethoven and of Bach, dissecting it, committing it to memory.'

Years later Miller called upon him and happened to see in his room a dilapidated copy of Beethoven's sonatas. Turning the leaves over, he noticed many indications on them of careful study, and remarked upon them to Wolf.

'Yes', said Wolf very seriously, 'those were bad days. I lived in a garret, and had no piano; so I used to take out the sonatas separately, and study them in the Prater.'

Ernest Newman, *Hugo Wolf*, New York: Dover Publications, 1966, p. 14.

In February 1883, Richard Wagner died. A year later *The Vienna Academic Wagner Society* sponsored an anniversary concert — *In Memory of Richard Wagner*. The celebrated virtuoso pianist Anton Rubinstein was invited to play a selection of Beethoven's piano sonatas. Hugo Wolf was in the audience and wrote a review of the recital — in characteristically trenchant terms — that gives an insight into Rubinstein's style of performance:

> 'Rubinstein moves among our ivory crushers like Gulliver among the Lilliputians ... As for Beethoven's sonatas, he must bow to [Hans von] Bülow, who, three years ago, played the last six sonatas for us, and so perfectly as to persuade us immediately that Beethoven should be played in this way and in no other. The dreadfully hurried tempi, the unexampled interpretive liberties, the nonchalance with which Rubinstein treats particularly prominent passages such as the recitative phrase in the first movement of the Sonata in D minor, etc., all these dark blemishes on the luminous glory of his heroic deeds. Perhaps it was simply not Anton Rubinstein's night for Beethoven?'

Henry Pleasants, editor and translator, *The Music Criticism of Hugo Wolf*, New York: Holmes & Meier Publishers, 1978, pp. 12–13.

BIBLIOGRAPHY

The author has individually consulted all the publications listed in this bibliography and can confirm that each makes reference, in some way or other, to Beethoven and his works. It will be evident from their titles which of these are publications devoted exclusively to the composer. Others that make only passing reference to Beethoven and his compositions, nevertheless unfailingly bear testimony to his genius and humanity. The diversity of the titles listed testifies to the centrality of Beethoven to western culture and beyond; the mere survey of these should be of itself a rewarding experience for a lover of so-called classical music. The entries are confined to book publications, reflecting the scope of the author's researches. The cut-off date for this was 2007; no works after this date are listed, notwithstanding the author is mindful that Beethoven musicology, and related publication, continue to be a major field of endeavour.

Abraham, Gerald. *Beethoven's second-period quartets*. London: Oxford University Press: Humphrey Milford, 1944.

Abraham, Gerald. *Essays on Russian and East European music*. Oxford: Clarendon Press: New York: Oxford University Press, 1985.

Abraham, Gerald, Editor. *The age of Beethoven, 1790-1830*. London: Oxford University Press, 1982.

Abraham, Gerald. *The tradition of Western music*. London: Oxford University Press, 1974.

Abse, Dannie and Joan. *The Music lover's literary companion*. London: Robson Books, 1988.

Adorno, Theodor W., Translator. *Alban Berg: master of the smallest link*. Cambridge: Cambridge University Press, 1991.

Adorno, Theodor W. *Beethoven: the philosophy of music; fragments and texts*. Cambridge: Polity Press, 1998.

Albrecht, Daniel, Editor. *Modernism and music: an anthology of sources*. Chicago; London: University of Chicago Press, 2004.

Albrecht, Theodore, Translator and Editor. *Letters to Beethoven and other correspondence*. Lincoln, New England: University of Nebraska Press, 3 vols., 1996.

Allsobrook, David Ian. *Liszt: my travelling circus life*. London: Macmillan, 1991.

Anderson, Christopher, Editor and Translator. *Selected writings of Max Reger*. New York; London: Routledge, 2006.

Anderson, Emily, Editor and Translator. *The letters of Beethoven*. London: Macmillan, 3 vols.,1961.

Anderson, Martin, Editor. *Klemperer on music: shavings from a musician's workbench*. London: Toccata Press, 1986.

Antheil, George. *Bad boy of music*. London; New York: Hurst & Blackett Ltd., 1945.

Appleby, David P. *Heitor Villa-Lobos: a bio-bibliography*. New York: Greenwood Press, 1988.

Aprahamian, Felix, Editor. *Essays on music: an anthology from The Listener*. London, Cassell, 1967.

Armero, Gonzalo and Jorge de Persia. *Manuel de Falla : his life & works*. London: Omnibus Press, 1999.

Arnold, Ben, Editor. *The Liszt companion*. Westport, Connecticut; London: Greenwood Press, 2002.

Arnold, Denis and Nigel Fortune, Editors. *The Beethoven companion*. London: Faber and Faber, 1973.

Ashbrook, William. *Donizetti*. London: Cassell, 1965.

Auner, Joseph Henry. *A Schoenberg reader: documents of a life*. New Haven Connecticut; London: Yale University Press, 2003.

Avins, Styra, Editor. *Johannes Brahms: life and letters*. Oxford: Oxford University Press, 1997.

Azoury, Pierre H. *Chopin through his contemporaries: friends, lovers, and rivals*. Westport, Connecticut: Greenwood Press, 1999.

Badura-Skoda, Paul. *Carl Czerny: On the Proper Performance of all Beethoven's Works for the Piano*. Universal Edition: A. G. Wien, 1970.

Bailey, Cyril. *Hugh Percy Allen*. London: Oxford University

Press, 1948.

Bailey, Kathryn. *The life of Webern.* Cambridge: Cambridge University Press, 1998.

Barenboim, Daniel. *A life in music.* London: Weidenfeld & Nicolson, 1991.

Barlow, Michael. *Whom the gods love: the life and music of George Butterworth.* London: Toccata Press, 1997.

Barrett-Ayres, Reginald. *Joseph Haydn and the string quartet.* New York: Schirmer Books, 1974.

Bartos, Frantisek. *Bedrich Smetana: Letters and reminiscences.* Prague: Artia, 1953.

Barzun, Jacques. *Pleasures of music: an anthology of writing about music and musicians.* London: Cassell, 1977.

Bauer-Lechner, Natalie. *Recollections of Gustav Mahler.* London: Faber Music, 1980.

Bazhanov, N. Nikolai. *Rakhmaninov.* Moscow: Raduga, 1983.

Beaumont, Antony, Editor. *Ferruccio Busoni: Selected letters.* London: Faber and Faber, 1987.

Beaumont, Antony, Editor. *Gustav Mahler, letters to his wife.* London: Faber and Faber, 2004.

Beecham, Thomas. *A mingled chime: an autobiography.* New York: Da Capo Press, 1976.

Bekker, Paul. *Beethoven.* London: J. M. Dent & Sons, 1925.

Bellasis, Edward. *Cherubini: memorials illustrative of his life.* London: Burns and Oates, 1874.

Bennett, James R. Sterndale. *The life of William Sterndale Bennett.* Cambridge: University Press, 1907.

Benser, Caroline Cepin. *Egon Wellesz (1885–1974): chronicle of twentieth-century musician.* New York: P. Lang, 1985.

Berlioz, Hector. *Evenings in the orchestra.* Harmondsworth: Penguin Books, 1963.

Berlioz, Hector. *The musical madhouse (Les grotesques de la musique).* Rochester, New York: University of Rochester Press, 2003.

Bernard, Jonathan W., Editor. *Elliott Carter: collected essays and lectures, 1937-1995.* Rochester, New York; Woodbridge: University of Rochester Press, 1998.

Bernstein, Leonard. *The joy of music.* New York: Simon and Schuster, 1959.

Bertensson, Sergei. *Sergei Rachmaninoff: a lifetime in music.* London: G. Allen & Unwin, 1965.

Biancolli, Louis. *The Flagstad manuscript.* New York: Putnam, 1952.

Bickley, Nora, Editor. *Letters from and to Joseph Joachim.* London: Macmillan, 1914.

Bie, Oskar. *A history of the pianoforte and pianoforte players.* New York: Da Capo Press, 1966.

Blaukopf, Herta. *Mahler's unknown letters.* London: Gollancz, 1986.

Blaukopf, Kurt and Herta. *Mahler: his life, work and world.* London: Thames and Hudson, 1991.

Bliss, Arthur. *As I remember.* London: Thames Publishing, 1989.

Block, Adrienne Fried. *Amy Beach, passionate Victorian: the life and work of an American composer, 1867–1944.* New York: Oxford University Press, 1998.

Bloch, Ernst. *Essays on the philoso-*

phy of music. Cambridge: Cambridge University Press, 1985.

Blocker, Robert. *The Robert Shaw reader*. New Haven; London: Yale University Press, 2004.

Blom, Eric. *A musical postbag*. London: J. M. Dent, 1945.

Blom, Eric. *Beethoven's pianoforte sonatas discussed*. London: J. M. Dent, 1938.

Blom, Eric. *Classics major and minor: with some other musical ruminations*. London: J. M. Dent, 1958.

Blum, David. *The art of quartet playing: the Guarneri Quartet in conversation with David Blum*. London: Gollancz, 1986.

Blume, Friedrich. *Classic and Romantic music: a comprehensive survey*. London: Faber and Faber, 1972.

Boden, Anthony. *The Parrys of the Golden Vale: background to genius*. London: Thames Publishing, 1998.

Bonavia, Ferruccio. *Musicians on music*. London: Routledge & Kegan Paul, 1956.

Bonds, Mark Evan *After Beethoven: imperatives of originality in the symphony*. Cambridge, Massachusetts; London: Harvard University Press, 1996.

Bonis, Ferenc, Editor. *The selected writings of Zoltán Kodály*. London; New York: Boosey & Hawkes, 1974.

Bookspan, Martin. *André Previn: a biography*. London: Hamilton, 1981.

Boros, James and Richard Toop, Editors. *Brian Ferneyhough: Collected writings*. Amsterdam: Harwood Academic, 1995.

Boulez, Pierre. *Stocktakings from an apprenticeship*. Oxford: Clarendon Press, 1991.

Boult, Adrian. *Boult on music: words from a lifetime's communication*. London: Toccata Press, 1983.

Boult, Adrian. *My own trumpet*. London, Hamish Hamilton, 1973.

Boult, Adrian with Jerrold Northrop Moore. *Music and friends: seven decades of letters to Adrian Boult from Elgar, Vaughan Williams, Holst, Bruno Walter, Yehudi Menuhin and other friends*. London: Hamish Hamilton, 1979.

Bovet, Marie Anne de. *Charles Gounod: his life and his works*. London: S. Low, Marston, Searle & Rivington, Ltd., 1891.

Bowen, Catherine Drinker. *Beloved friend: the story of Tchaikowsky and Nadejda von Meck*. London: Hutchinson & Co., 1937.

Bowen, Meiron, Editor. *Gerhard on music: selected writings*. Brookfield, Vermont: Ashgate, 2000.

Bowen, Meirion. *Michael Tippett*. London: Robson Books, 1982.

Bowen, Meiron, Editor. *Music of the angels: essays and sketchbooks of Michael Tippett*. London: Eulenburg, 1980.

Bowen, Meiron, Editor. *Tippett on music*. Oxford: Clarendon Press, 1995.

Bowers, Faubion. *Scriabin: a biography*. Mineola: Dover; London: Constable, 1996.

Boyden, Matthew. *Richard Strauss*. London: Weidenfeld & Nicolson, 1999.

Bozarth, George S., Editor. *Brahms studies: analytical and historical* perspectives; papers delivered at the International Brahms Conference, Washington, DC, 5-8 May 1983. Oxford: Clarendon Press, 1990.

Brand, Juliane, Christopher Hailey and Donald Harris, Editors. *The Berg-Schoenberg correspondence: selected letters.* Basingstoke: Macmillan, 1987.

Brandenbugh, Sieghard, Editor. *Haydn, Mozart, & Beethoven: studies in the music of the classical period: essays in honor of Alan Tyson.* Oxford: Clarendon Press, 1998.

Braunstein, Joseph. *Musica Æterna, program notes for 1961–1971.* New York: Musica Æterna, 1972.

Braunstein, Joseph. *Musica Æterna, program notes for 1971–1976.* New York: Musica Æterna, 1978.

Brendel, Alfred. *Alfred Brendel on music: collected essays.* Chicago, Illinois: A Cappella Books, 2001.

Brendel, Alfred. *The veil of order: Alfred Brendel in conversation with Martin Meyer.* London: Faber and Faber, 2002.

Breuning, Gerhard von. *Memories of Beethoven: from the house of the black-robed Spaniards.* Cambridge: Cambridge University Press, 1992.

Briscoe, James R., Editor. (Brief Description): *Debussy in performance.* New Haven: Yale University Press, 1999.

Brott, Alexander Betty Nygaard King. *Alexander Brott: my lives in music.* Oakville, Ontario; Niagara Falls, New York: Mosaic Press, 2005.

Brown, Alfred Peter. *The symphonic repertoire. Vol. 2, The first golden age of the Viennese symphony: Haydn, Mozart, Beethoven, and Schubert.* Bloomington, Indiana: Indiana University Press, 2002.

Brown, Maurice John Edwin. *Schubert: a critical biography.* London: Macmillan; New York: St. Martin's Press, 1958.

Broyles, Michael. *Beethoven: the emergence and evolution of Beethoven's heroic style.* New York: Excelsior Music Publishing Co., 1987.

Brubaker, Bruce and Jane Gottlieb, Editors. *Pianist, scholar, connoisseur: essays in honor of Jacob Lateiner.* Stuyvesant, N.Y., Pendragon Press, 2000.

Buch, Esteban. *Beethoven's Ninth: a political history.* Chicago; London: University of Chicago Press, 2003.

Burk, John N., Editor. *Letters of Richard Wagner: the Burrell collection.* London: Gollancz, 1951.

Burnham, Scott G. *Beethoven hero.* Princeton, New Jersey: Princeton University Press, 1995.

Burnham, Scott G and Michael P. Steinberg, Editors. *Beethoven and his world.* Princeton, New Jersey; Oxford: Princeton University Press, 2000.

Burton, William Westbrook, Editor. *Conversations about Bernstein.* New York; Oxford: Oxford University Press, 1995.

Busch, Fritz. *Pages from a musician's life.* London: Hogarth Press, 1953.

Busch, Hans, Editor. *Verdi's Aida: the history of an opera in letters and documents.* Minneapolis:

University of Minnesota Press, 1978.

Busch, Hans, Editor. *Verdi's Falstaff in letters and contemporary reviews.* Bloomington: Indiana University Press, 1997.

Busch, Marie, Translator. *Memoirs of Eugenie Schumann.* London: W. Heinemann, 1927.

Bush, Alan Dudley. *In my eighth decade and other essays.* London: Kahn & Averill, 1980.

Busoni, Ferruccio. *Letters to his wife.* Translated by Rosamond Ley. New York: Da Capo Press, 1975.

Byron, Reginald. *Music, culture, & experience: selected papers of John Blacking.* Chicago: University of Chicago Press, 1995.

Cairns, David. *Responses: musical essays and reviews.* New York: Da Capo Press, 1980.

Cardus, Neville. *Talking of music.* London: Collins, 1957.

Carley, Lionel. *Delius: a life in letters.* London: Scolar Press in association with the Delius Trust, 1988.

Carley, Lionel. *Grieg and Delius: a chronicle of their friendship in letters.* London: Marion Boyars, 1993.

Carner, Mosco. *Major and minor.* London: Duckworth, 1980

Carner, Mosco. *Puccini: a critical biography.* London: Duckworth, 1958.

Carroll, Brendan G. *The last prodigy: a biography of Erich Wolfgang Korngold.* Portland, Oregon: Amadeus Press, 1997.

Carse, Adam von Ahn. *The life of Jullien: adventurer, showman-conductor and establisher of the Promenade Concerts in England, together with a history of those concerts up to 1895.* Cambridge England: Heffer, 1951.

Carse, Adam von Ahn. *The orchestra from Beethoven to Berlioz: a history of the orchestra in the first half of the 19th century, and of the development of orchestral baton-conducting.* Cambridge: W. Heffer, 1948.

Casals, Pablo. *Joys and sorrows: reflections by Pablo Casals as told to Albert E. Kahn.* London: Macdonald, 1970.

Casals, Pablo. *The memoirs of Pablo Casals as told to Thomas Dozier.* London: Life en Español, 1959.

Chappell, Paul. *Dr. S. S. Wesley, 1810–1876: portrait of a Victorian musician.* Great Wakering: Mayhew-McCrimmon, 1977.

Chasins, Abram. *Leopold Stokowski, a profile.* New York: Hawthorn Books, 1979.

Charlton, Davi, Editor and Martyn Clarke Translator. *E.T.A. Hoffmann's musical writings: Kreisleriana, The Poet and the Composer.* Cambridge: Cambridge University Press, 1989.

Chávez, Carlos. *Musical thought.* Cambridge: Harvard University Press, 1961.

Chesterman, Robert, Editor. *Conversations with conductors: Bruno Walter, Sir Adrian Boult, Leonard Bernstein, Ernest Ansermet, Otto Klemperer, Leopold Stokowski.* Totowa, New Jersey: Rowman and Littlefield, 1976.

Chissell, Joan. *Clara Schumann: a dedicated spirit; a study of her life and work.* London: Hamilton, 1983.

Chua, Daniel K. L. *The "Galitzin" quartets of Beethoven: Opp.127, 132, 130.* Princeton: Princeton

University Press, 1995.

Citron, Marcia, Editor. *The letters of Fanny Hensel to Felix Mendelssohn.* Stuyvesant, New York: Pendragon Press, 1987.

Clark, Walter Aaron. *Enrique Granados: poet of the piano.* Oxford, England; New York, N.Y.: Oxford University Press, 2006.

Clark, Walter Aaron. *Isaac Albéniz: portrait of a romantic.* Oxford; New York: Oxford University Press, 1999.

Clive, Peter. *Beethoven and his world.* Oxford University Press, 2001.

Closson, Ernest. *History of the piano.* Translated by Delano Ames and edited by Robin Golding. London: Paul Elek, 1947.

Cockshoot, John V. *The fugue in Beethoven's piano music.* London: Routledge & Kegan Paul, 1959.

Coe, Richard N, Translator. *Life of Rossini by Stendhal.* London: Calder & Boyars, 1970.

Coleman, Alexander, Editor. *Diversions & animadversions: essays from The new criterion.* New Brunswick, New Jersey; London: Transaction Publishers, 2005.

Colerick, George. *From the Italian girl to Cabaret: musical humour, parody and burlesque.* London: Juventus, 1998.

Coleridge, A. D. *Life of Moscheles, with selections from his diaries and correspondence by his wife.* London: Hurst & Blackett, 1873.

Colles, Henry Cope. *Essays and lectures.* London: Humphrey Milford, Oxford University Press, 1945.

Cone, Edward T., Editor. *Roger Sessions on music: collected essays.* Princeton, New Jersey: Princeton University Press, 1979.

Cone, Edward T. *The composer's voice.* Berkeley; London: University of California Press, 1974.

Cook, Susan and Judy S. Tsou, Editors. *Cecilia reclaimed: feminist perspectives on gender and music.* Urbana: University of Illinois Press, 1994.

Cooper, Barry. *Beethoven.* The master musicians series. Oxford: Oxford University Press, 2000.

Cooper, Barry. *Beethoven and the creative process.* Oxford: Clarendon Press, 1990.

Cooper, Barry. *Beethoven's folksong settings: chronology, sources, style.* Cambridge: Cambridge University Press, 1991.

Cooper, Barry. *The Beethoven compendium: a guide to Beethoven's life and music.* London: Thames and Hudson, 1991.

Cooper, Martin. *Beethoven: the last decade, 1817–1827.* London: Oxford University Press, 1970.

Cooper, Martin. *Judgements of value: selected writings on music.* Oxford; New York: Oxford University Press, 1988.

Cooper, Martin. *Ideas and music.* London: Barrie and Rockliff, 1965.

Cooper, Victoria L. *The house of Novello: the practice and policy of a Victorian music publisher, 1829–1866.* Aldershot, Hants: Ashgate, 2003.

Coover, James. *Music at auction: Puttick and Simpson (of London), 1794–1971: being an annotated, chronological list of sales of musical materials.* Warren, Michigan: Harmonie Park Press, 1988.

Copland, Aaron. *Copland on music*. London: Deutsch, 1961.

Corredor, J. Ma. *Conversations with Casals*. London: Hutchinson, 1956.

Cott, Jonathan. *Stockhausen: conversations with the composer*. London: Picador, 1974.

Cottrell, Stephen. *Professional music making in London: ethnography and experience*. Aldershot: Ashgate, 2004.

Cowell, Henry. *Charles Ives and his music*. New York: Oxford University Press, 1955.

Cowling, Elizabeth. *The cello*. London: Batsford, 1983.

Crabbe, John. *Beethoven's empire of the mind*. Newbury: Lovell Baines, 1982.

Craft, Robert. *An improbable life: memoirs*. Nashville: Vanderbilt University Press, 2002.

Craft, Robert, Editor. *Stravinsky: selected correspondence*. London: Faber and Faber, 3 Vols. 1982–1985.

Craw, Howard Allen. *A biography and thematic catalog of the works of J. L. Dussek: 1760–1812*. Ann Arbor: Michigan, 1965.

Crawford, Richard, R. Allen Lott and Carol J. Oja, Editors. *A Celebration of American music: words and music in honor of H. Wiley Hitchcock*. Ann Arbor: University of Michigan Press, 1990.

Craxton, Harold and Tovey, Donald Francis. *Beethoven: Sonatas for Pianoforte*. London: The Associated Board, [1931].

Crichton, Ronald: Editor. *The memoirs of Ethel Smyth*. New York: Viking, 1987.

Crist, Stephen A. and Roberta M. Marvin, Editors. *Historical musicology: sources, methods, interpretations*. Rochester, New York: University of Rochester Press, 2004.

Crofton, Ian and Donald Fraser, Editors. *A dictionary of musical quotations*. London: Croom Helm, 1985.

Crompton, Louis, Editor. *Shaw, Bernard: The great composers: reviews and bombardments*. Berkeley; London: University of California Press, 1978.

Csicserry-Ronay, Elizabeth, Translator and Editor. *Hector Berlioz: The art of music and other essays: (A travers chants)*. Bloomington: Indiana University Press, 1994.

Curtiss, Mina Kirstein. *Bizet and his world*. London: Secker & Warburg, 1959.

Cuyler, Louise Elvira. *The symphony*. New York: Harcourt Brace Jovanovich, 1973.

Dahlhaus, Carl. *Ludwig van Beethoven: approaches to his music*. Oxford: Clarendon Press, 1991.

Dahlhaus, Carl. *Nineteenth-century music*. Translated by J. Bradford Robinson. Berkeley; London: University of California Press, 1989.

Daniels, Robin. *Conversations with Cardus*. London: Gollancz, 1976.

Daniels, Robin. Conversations with Menuhin. London: Macdonald General Books, 1979.

Day, James. *Vaughan Williams*. London: Dent, 1961.

Davies, Peter Maxwell. *Studies from two decades*. Selected and introduced by Stephen Pruslin.

London: Boosey & Hawkes, 1979.

Dean, Winton. *Georges Bizet: his life and work*. London: J.M. Dent, 1965.

Deas, Stewart. *In defence of Hanslick*. London: Williams and Norgate, 1940.

Debussy, Claude. *Debussy on music*. London: Secker & Warburg, 1977.

Delbanco, Nicholas. *The Beaux Arts Trio*. London: Gollancz, 1985.

Demény, Janos, Editor. *Béla Bartók: letters*. London: Faber and Faber, 1971.

Dent, Edward Joseph. *Selected essays*. Edited by Hugh Taylor. Cambridge; New York: Cambridge University Press, 1979.

Deutsch, Otto Erich. *Mozart: a documentary biography*. London: Adam & Charles Black, 1965.

Deutsch, Otto Erich. *Schubert: a documentary biography*. London: J.M. Dent, 1946

Deutsch, Otto Erich. *Schubert: memoirs by his friends*. London: Adam & Charles Black, 1958.

Dibble, Jeremy. *C. Hubert H. Parry: his life and music*. Oxford: Clarendon Press, 1992.

Dibble, Jeremy. *Charles Villiers Stanford: man and musician*. Oxford: Oxford University Press, 2002.

Donakowski, Conrad L. *A muse for the masses: ritual and music in an age of democratic revolution, 1770–1870*. Chicago: University of Chicago Press, 1977.

Dower, Catherine. *Alfred Einstein on music: selected music criticisms*. New York: Greenwood Press, 1991.

Downs, Philip G. *Classical music: the era of Haydn, Mozart, and Beethoven*. New York: W.W. Norton, 1992.

Drabkin, William. *Beethoven: Missa Solemnis*. Cambridge: Cambridge University Press, 1991.

Dreyfus, Kay. *The farthest north of humanness: letters of Percy Grainger, 1901–1914*. South Melbourne; Basingstoke: Macmillan, 1985.

Dubal, David, Editor. *Remembering Horowitz: 125 pianists recall a legend*. New York: Schirmer Books, 1993.

Dubal, David. *The world of the concert pianist*. London: Victor Gollancz, 1985.

Dvořák, Otakar. *Antonín Dvořák, my father*. Spillville, Iowa: Czech Historical Research Center, 1993.

Dyson, George. *The progress of music*. London: Oxford University Press, Humphrey Milford, 1932.

Eastaugh, Kenneth. *Havergal Brian: the making of a composer*. London: Harrap, 1976.

Edwards, Allen. *Flawed words and stubborn sounds: a conversation with Elliott Carter*. New York: Norton & Company, 1971.

Edwards, Frederick George. *Musical haunts in London*. London: J. Curwen & Sons, 1895.

Ehrlich, Cyril. *First philharmonic: a history of the Royal Philharmonic Society*. Oxford: Clarendon Press, 1995.

Einstein, Alfred. *A short history of music*. London: Cassell and Company Ltd., 1948.

Einstein, Alfred. *Essays on music*. London: Faber and Faber, 1958.

Einstein, Alfred. *Mozart: his character, his work*. London: Cassell and Company Ltd., 1946.

Einstein, Alfred. *Music in the Romantic era*. London: J.M. Dent Ltd., 1947.

Ekman, Karl. *Jean Sibelius, his life and personality*. New York: Tudor Publishing. Co., 1945.

Elgar, Edward. *A future for English music: and other lectures*, Edited by Percy M. Young. London: Dobson, 1968.

Elkin, Robert. *Queen's Hall, 1893–1941*. London: Rider, 1944.

Ella, John. *Musical sketches, abroad and at home: with original music by Mozart, Czerny, Graun, etc., vocal cadenzas and other musical illustrations*. London: Ridgway, Vol. 1., 1869.

Ellis, William Ashton. *The family letters of Richard Wagner*. Edited and translated by William Ashton Ellis and enlarged with introduction and notes by John Deathridge. Basingstoke: Macmillan, 1991.

Ellis, William Ashton. *Richard Wagner's prose works: Vol. 1, The art-work of the future*. Edited and translated by William Ashton Ellis. London: Kegan Paul, Trench, Trübner, 1895.

Ellis, William Ashton. *Richard Wagner's prose works: Vol. 2, Opera and drama*. Edited and translated by William Ashton Ellis. London: Kegan Paul, Trench, Trübner, 1900.

Ellis, William Ashton. *Richard Wagner's prose works: Vol. 3, The theatre*. Edited and translated by William Ashton Ellis. London: Kegan Paul, Trench, Trübner, 1907.

Ellis, William Ashton. *Richard Wagner's prose works: Vol. 4, Art and politics*. Edited and translated by William Ashton Ellis. London: Kegan Paul, Trench, Trübner, 1895.

Ellis, William Ashton. *Richard Wagner's prose works: Vol. 5, Actors and singers*. Edited and translated by William Ashton Ellis. London: Kegan Paul, Trench, Trübner, 1896.

Ellis, William Ashton. *Richard Wagner's prose works: Vol. 6, Religion and art*. Edited and translated by William Ashton Ellis. London: Kegan Paul, Trench, Trübner, 1897.

Ellis, William Ashton. *Richard Wagner's prose works: Vol. 7, In Paris and Dresden*. Edited and translated by William Ashton Ellis. London: Kegan Paul, Trench, Trübner, 1898.

Ellis, William Ashton. *Richard Wagner's prose works: Vol. 8, Posthumous*. Edited and translated by William Ashton Ellis. London: Kegan Paul, Trench, Trübner, 1899.

Elterlein, Ernst von. *Beethoven's pianoforte sonatas: explained for the lovers of the musical art*. London: W. Reeves, 1898.

Engel, Carl. *Musical myths and facts*. London: Novello, Ewer & Co.; New York: J.L. Peters, 1876.

Eosze, László. *Zoltán Kodály: his life and work*. London: Collet's, 1962.

Etter, Brian K. *From classicism to modernism: Western musical culture and the metaphysics of order*. Aldershot: Ashgate, 2001.

Ewen, David. *From Bach to Stravinsky: the history of music by its foremost critics*. New York, Greenwood Press, 1968.

Ewen, David. *Romain Rolland's Essays on music*. New York: Dover Publications, 1959.

Fay, Amy. *Music-study in Germany: from the home correspondence of Amy Fay*. New York: Dover Publications, 1965.

Fenby, Eric. *Delius as I knew him*. London: Quality Press, 1936.

Ferguson, Donald Nivison. *Masterworks of the orchestral repertoire: a guide for listeners*. Minneapolis: University of Minnesota Press, 1954.

Fétis, François-Joseph. *Curiosités historiques de la musique: complément nécessaire de la Musique mise à la portée de tout le monde*. Paris: Janet et Cotelle, 1830.

Fifield, Christopher. *Max Bruch: his life and works*. London: Gollancz, 1988.

Fifield, Christopher. *True artist and true friend: a biography of Hans Richter*. Oxford: Clarendon Press, 1993.

Finson, Jon and R. Larry Todd, Editors. *Mendelssohn and Schumann: essays on their music and its context*. Durham, N.C.: Duke University Press, 1984.

Fischer, Edwin. *Beethoven's pianoforte sonatas: a guide for students & amateurs*. London: Faber and Faber, 1959.

Fischer, Edwin. *Reflections on music*. London: Williams and Norgate, 1951.

Fischer, Hans Conrad and Erich Kock. *Ludwig van Beethoven: a study in text and pictures*. London: Macmillan; New York, St. Martin's Press, 1972.

Fischmann, Zdenka E. *Janác̆ek-Newmarch correspondence*. 1st limited and numbered edition. Rockville, MD: Kabel Publishers, 1986.

Fitzlyon, April. *Maria Malibran: diva of the romantic age*. London: Souvenir Press, 1987.

FitzLyon, April. *The price of genius: a life of Pauline Viardot*. London: John Calder, 1964.

Forbes, Elliot, Editor. *Thayer's life of Beethoven*. Princeton, New Jersey: Princeton University Press, 1967.

Foreman, Lewis. *Bax: a composer and his times*. London: Scolar Press, 1983.

Foreman, Lewis, Editor. *Farewell, my youth, and other writings by Arnold Bax*. Aldershot: Scolar Press, 1992.

Foster, Myles Birket. *History of the Philharmonic Society of London, 1813–1912: a record of a hundred years' work in the cause of music*. London: Bodley Head, 1912.

Foulds, John. *Music today: its heritage from the past, and legacy to the future*. London: I. Nicholson and Watson, limited, 1934.

Frank, Mortimer H. *Arturo Toscanini: the NBC years*. Portland, Oregon: Amadeus Press, 2002.

Fraser, Andrew Alastair. *Essays on music*. London: Oxford University Press, H. Milford, 1930.

Frohlich, Martha. *Beethoven's Appassionata' sonata*. Oxford: Clarendon Press, 1991.

Gal, Hans. *The golden age of Vienna*. London: Max Parrish & Co. Limited, 1948.

Gal, Hans. *The musician's world: great composers in their letters*. London: Thames and Hudson,

Galatopoulos, Stelios. *Bellini: life, times, music.* London: Sanctuary, 2002.

Garden, Edward and Nigel Gottrei, Editors.

'To my best friend': correspondence between Tchaikovsky and Nadezhda von Meck, 1876–1878. Oxford: Clarendon Press, 1993.

Geck, Martin. Beethoven. London: Haus, 2003.

Gerig, Reginald. *Famous pianists & their technique.* Washington: R. B. Luce, 1974.

Gilliam, Bryan. *The life of Richard Strauss.* Cambridge: Cambridge University Press, 1999.

Gilliam, Bryan, Editor. *Richard Strauss and his world.* Princeton, New Jersey: Princeton University Press, 1992.

Gillies, Malcolm and Bruce Clunies Ross, Editors. *Grainger on music.* Oxford; New York: Oxford University Press, 1999.

Gillies, Malcolm and David Pear, Editors. *The all-round man: selected letters of Percy Grainger, 1914–1961.* Oxford: Clarendon Press, 1994.

Gillies, Malcolm, Editor. *The Bartók companion.* London: Faber and Faber, 1993.

Gillmor, Alan M. *Erik Satie.* Basingstoke: Macmillan Press, 1988.

Glehn, M. E. *Goethe and Mendelssohn : (1821–1831).* London: Macmillan, 1874.

Glowacki, John, Editor. *Paul A. Pisk: Essays in his honor.* Austin, Texas: University of Texas, 1966

Gollancz, Victor. *Journey towards music: a memoir.* London: Victor Gollancz Ltd., 1964.

Good, Edwin Marshall. *Giraffes, black dragons, and other pianos: a technological history from Cristofori to the modern concert grand.* Stanford, California: Stanford University Press, 1982.

Gordon, David. *Musical visitors to Britain.* London: Routledge, 2005.

Gordon, Stewart. *A history of keyboard literature: music for the piano and its forerunners.* Schirmer Books: New York: London : Prentice Hall International, 1996.

Gorrell, Lorraine. *The nineteenth-century German lied.* Portland, Oregon: Amadeus Press, 1993.

Goss, Glenda D. *Jean Sibelius: the Hämeenlinna letters: scenes from a musical life, 1875–1895.* Esbo, Finland: Schildts, 1997.

Goss, Madeleine. *Bolero: the life of Maurice Ravel.* New York: Tudor, 1945.

Gotch, Rosamund Brunel, Editor. *Mendelssohn and his friends in Kensington: letters from Fanny and Sophy Horsley, written 1833–36.* London: Oxford University Press, 1938.

Gounod, Charles. *Charles Gounod; autobiographical reminiscences: with family letters and notes on music; from the French.* London: William Heinemann, 1896.

Grabs, Manfred, Editor. *Hanns Eisler: a rebel in music; selected writings.* Berlin: Seven Seas Publishers, 1978.

Grace, Harvey. *A musician at large.* London: Oxford University Press, H. Milford, 1928.

(La) Grange, Henry-Louis de. *Gustav*

Mahler. Oxford: Oxford University Press, 1995.

Graves, Charles L. *Hubert Parry: his life and works*. London: Macmillan, 1926.

Graves, Charles L. *Post-Victorian music: with other studies and sketches*. London: Macmillan and Co., limited, 1911.

Graves, Charles L. *The life & letters of Sir George Grove, Hon. D.C.L. (Durham), Hon. LL.D. (Glasgow), formerly director of the Royal college of music*. London: Macmillan and Co., Ltd.; New York: The Macmillan Co., 1903.

Gray, Cecil. *Musical chairs, or, between two stools: being the life and memoirs of Cecil Gray*. London: Home & Van Thal, 1948.

Gregor-Dellin and Dietrich Mack, Editors. *Cosima Wagner's diaries.: Vol. 1, 1869 – 1877*. London: Collins, 1978-1980.

Griffiths, Paul. *Modern music: the avant-garde since 1945*. London: J. M. Dent & Sons Ltd., 1981.

Griffiths, Paul. *Olivier Messiaen and the music of time*. London: Faber and Faber, 1985.

Griffiths, Paul. *Peter Maxwell Davies*. London: Robson Books, 1988.

Griffiths, Paul. *The sea on fire: Jean Barraqué*. Rochester, New York: Woodbridge: University of Rochester Press, 2003.

Griffiths, Paul. *The string quartet*. London: Thames and Hudson, 1983.

Grout, Donald Jay and Claude V. Palisca, Editors. *A history of Western music*. London: J. M. Dent, 1988.

Grove, George. *Beethoven and his nine symphonies*. London: Novello, Ewer, 1896.

Grover, Ralph Scott. *Ernest Chausson: the man and his music*. London: The Athlone Press, 1980.

Grover, Ralph Scott. *The music of Edmund Rubbra*. Aldershot: Scolar Press, 1993.

Grun, Bernard. *Alban Berg: letters to his wife*. Edited and translated by Bernard Grun. London: Faber and Faber, 1971.

Gutman, David. *Prokofiev*. London: Omnibus Press, 1990.

Hadow, William Henry. *Collected essays*. London: H. Milford at the Oxford University Press, 1928.

Hadow, William Henry. *Beethoven's Op. 18 Quartets*. London: H. Milford at the Oxford University Press, 1926.

Haggin, Bernard H. *Music observed*. New York: Oxford University Press, 1964.

Hailey, Christopher. *Franz Schreker, 1878–1934: a cultural biography*. Cambridge: Cambridge University Press, 1993.

Hall, Michael. *Leaving home: a conducted tour of twentieth-century music with Simon Rattle*. London: Faber and Faber, 1996.

Hall, Patricia and Friedemann Sallis, Editors. (Brief Description): *A handbook to twentieth-century musical sketches*. Cambridge: Cambridge University Press, 2004.

Hallé, C. E. *Life and letters of Sir Charles Hallé: being an autobiography (1819–1860) with correspondence and diaries*. London: Smith, Elder & Co., 1896.

Halstead, Jill. *The woman composer: creativity and the gendered politics of musical composition*. Aldershot: Ashgate, 1997.

Hamburger, Michael, Editor and Translator. *Beethoven letters, journals, and conversations*. New York: Thames and Hudson, 1951.

Hammelmann, Hanns A. and Ewald Osers. *The correspondence between Richard Strauss and Hugo von Hofmannsthal*. London: Collins, 1961.

Hanson, Lawrence and Elisabeth Hanson. *Tchaikovsky: the man behind the music*. New York: Dodd, Mead & Co, 1967.

Harding, James. *Massenet*. London: J. M. Dent & Sons Ltd., 1970.

Harding, James. *Saint-Saëns and his circle*. London: Chapman & Hall, 1965.

Harding, Rosamond E. M. *Origins of musical time and expression*. London: Oxford University Press, 1938.

Harman, Alec with Anthony Milner and Wilfrid Mellers. *Man and his music: the story of musical experience in the West*. London: Barrie & Jenkins, 1988.

Harper, Nancy Lee. *Manuel de Falla: his life and music*. Lanham, Maryland; London: The Scarecrow Press, 2005.

Hartmann, Arthur.

'Claude Debussy as I knew him' *and other writings of Arthur Hartmann*. Edited by Samuel Hsu, Sidney Grolnic, and Mark Peters. Rochester, New York; Woodbridge: University of Rochester Press, 2003.

Haugen, Einar and Camilla Cai. *Ole Bull: Norway's romantic musician and cosmopolitan patriot*. Madison: The University of Wisconsin Press, 1993.

Headington, Christopher. *The Bodley Head history of Western music*. London: The Bodley Head, 1974.

Heartz, Daniel. *Music in European capitals: the galant style, 1720–1780*. New York; London: W. W. Norton, 2003.

Hedley, Arthur, Editor. *Selected correspondence of Fryderyk Chopin: abridged from Fryderyk Chopin's correspondence*. London: Heinemann, 1962.

Heiles, Anne Mischakoff. *Mischa Mischakoff: journeys of a concertmaster*. Sterling Heights, Michigan: Harmonie Park Press, 2006.

Henderson, Sanya Shoilevska. *Alex North, film composer: a biography, with musical analyses of a Streetcar named desire, Spartacus, The misfits, Under the volcano, and Prizzi's honor*. Jefferson, N.C.; London: McFarland, 2003.

Henschel, George. *Personal recollections of Johannes Brahms: some of his letters to and pages from a journal kept by George Henschel*. Boston: R G. Badger, 1907.

Henze, Hans Werner. *Bohemian fifths: an autobiography*. London: Faber and Faber, 1998.

Henze, Hans Werner. *Music and politics: collected writings 1953–81*. London: Faber and Faber, 1982.

Herbert, May, Translator. *Early letters of Robert Schumann*. London: George Bell and Sons, 1888.

Heyman, Barbara B. *Samuel Barber: the composer and his music*. New York: Oxford University Press, 1992.

Heyworth, Peter. *Otto Klemperer, his life and times*. Cambridge: Cambridge University Press, 2 Vols. 1983–1996.

Hildebrandt, Dieter. *Pianoforte: a social history of the piano*. London: Hutchinson, 1988.

Hill, Peter. *The Messiaen companion*. London: Faber and Faber, 1995.

Hill, Peter and Nigel Simeone. Messiaen. New Haven Connecticut; London: Yale University Press, 2005.

Hiller, Ferdinand. *Mendelssohn: Letters and recollections*. New York: Vienna House, 1972.

Hines, Robert Stephan. *The orchestral composer's point of view: essays on twentieth-century music by those who wrote it*. Norman: University of Oklahoma Press, 1970.

Ho, Allan B. *Shostakovich reconsidered*. London: Toccata Press, 1998.

Hodeir, André. *Since Debussy: a view of contemporary music*. New York: Da Capo Press, 1975.

Holmes, Edward. *The life of Mozart: including his correspondence*. London: Chapman and Hall, 1845.

Holmes, John L. *Composers on composers*. New York: Greenwood Press, 1990.

Hopkins, Antony. *The concertgoer's companion*. London: J.M. Dent & Sons Ltd., 1984.

Hopkins, Antony. *The seven concertos of Beethoven*. Aldershot: Scolar Press, 1996.

Holt, Richard. *Nicolas Medtner (1879–1951): a tribute to his art and personality*. London: D. Dobson, 1955.

Honegger, Arthur. *I am a composer*. London: Faber and Faber, 1966.

Hoover, Kathleen and John Cage. *Virgil Thomson: his life and music*. New York; London: T. Yoseloff, 1959.

Horgan, Paul. *Encounters with Stravinsky: a personal record*. London: The Bodley Head, 1972.

Horowitz, Joseph. *Conversations with Arrau*. London: Collins, 1982.

Horowitz, Joseph. Understanding Toscanini. London: Faber and Faber, 1987.

Horwood, Wally. *Adolphe Sax, 1814–1894: his life and legacy*. Bramley: Bramley Books, 1980.

Howie, Crawford. *Anton Bruckner: a documentary biography*. Lewiston, N.Y.; Lampeter: Edwin Mellen Press, 2002.

Hueffer, Francis. *Correspondence of Wagner and Liszt*. New York: Greenwood Press, 2 Vols. 1969.

Hughes, Spike. *The Toscanini legacy: a critical study of Arturo Toscanini's performances of Beethoven, Verdi, and other composers*. London: Putnam, 1959.

Hullah, Annette. *Theodor Leschetizky*. London and New York: J. Land & Co., 1906.

Le Huray, Peter and James Day, Editors. *Music and aesthetics in the eighteenth and early-nineteenth centuries*. Cambridge: Cambridge University Press, 1988.

D'Indy, Vincent. *César Franck*. New York: Dover Publications, 1965.

Jacobs, Arthur. *Arthur Sullivan: A Victorian musician.* Aldershot: Scolar Press, 1992.

Jahn, Otto. *Life of Mozart.* London: Novello, Ewer & Co., 1882.

Jefferson, Alan. *Sir Thomas Beecham: a centenary tribute.* London: World Records Ltd., 1979.

Jezic, Diane. *The musical migration and Ernst Toch.* Ames: Iowa State University Press, 1989.

Johnson, Douglas Porter, Editor. *The Beethoven sketchbooks: history, reconstruction, inventory.* Oxford: Clarendon, 1985.

Johnson, Stephen. *Bruckner remembered.* London: Faber and Faber, 1998.

Jones, David, Wyn. *Beethoven: Pastoral symphony.* Cambridge: Cambridge University Press, 1995.

Jones, David Wyn. *The life of Beethoven.* Cambridge: Cambridge University Press, 1998.

Jones, David Wyn. *The symphony in Beethoven's Vienna.* Cambridge: Cambridge University Press, 2006.

Jones, J. Barrie, Editor. *Gabriel Fauré: a life in letters.* London: Batsford, 1989.

Jones, Peter Ward, Editor and Translator. *The Mendelssohns on honeymoon: the 1837 diary of Felix and Cécile Mendelssohn Bartholdy, together with letters to their families.* Oxford: Clarendon Press, 1997.

Jones, Timothy. *Beethoven, the Moonlight and other sonatas, Op. 27 and Op. 31.* Cambridge; New York, N.Y.: Cambridge University Press, 1999.

Kalischer, A. C., Editor. *Beethoven's letters: a critical edition.* London: J. M. Dent, 1909.

Kárpáti, János. *Bartók's chamber music.* Stuyvesant, New York: Pendragon Press, 1994.

Keefe, Simon P. *The Cambridge companion to the concerto.* Cambridge, New York, N.Y.: Cambridge University Press, 2005.

Keller, Hans. *The great Haydn quartets: their interpretation.* London: J. M. Dent, 1986.

Keller, Hans, Editor. *The memoirs of Carl Flesch.* New York: Macmillan, 1958.

Keller, Hans, and Christopher Wintle. *Beethoven's string quartets in F minor, Op. 95 and C minor, Op. 131: two studies.* Nottingham: Department of Music, University of Nottingham, 1995.

Kelly, Thomas Forrest. *First nights at the opera: five musical premiers.* New Haven: Yale University Press, 2004.

Kennedy, Michael. *Adrian Boult.* London: Hamish Hamilton, 1987.

Kennedy, Michael. *Barbirolli, conductor laureate: the authorised biography.* London: Hart-Davis, MacGibbon, 1973.

Kennedy, Michael, Editor. *The autobiography of Charles Hallé; with correspondence and diaries.* London: Paul Elek, 1972.

Kennedy, Michael. *Hallé tradition: a century of music.* Manchester: Manchester University Press, 1960.

Kennedy, Michael. *The works of Ralph Vaughan Williams.* London: Oxford University Press, 1964.

Kemp, Ian. *Tippett: the composer and his music.* London; New York: Eulenburg Books, 1984.

Kerman, Joseph. *The Beethoven quartets.* London: Oxford University Press, 1967, c1966.

Kerman, Joseph. *Write all these down: essays on music.* Berkeley, California; London: University of California Press, 1994.

Kildea, Paul, Editor. *Britten on music.* Oxford: Oxford University Press, 2003.

Kinderman, William. *Beethoven.* Oxford: Oxford University Press, 1997.

Kinderman, William. *Beethoven's Diabelli variations.* Oxford: Clarendon Press; New York: Oxford University Press, 1987.

Kinderman, William, Editor. *The string quartets of Beethoven.* Urbana, Ilinois: University of Illinois Press, 2005.

King, Alec Hyatt. *Musical pursuits: selected essays.* London: British Library, 1987.

Kirby, F. E. *Music for piano: a short history.* Amadeus Press: Portland, 1995.

Kirkpatrick, John, Editor. *Charles E. Ives: Memos.* New York: W.W. Norton, 1972.

Knapp, Raymond. *Brahms and the challenge of the symphony.* Stuyvesant, N.Y.: Pendragon Press, c.1997.

Knight, Frida. *Cambridge music: from the Middle Ages to modern times.* Cambridge, England.: New York: Oleander Press, 1980.

Knight, Max, Translator. *A confidential matter: the letters of Richard Strauss and Stefan Zweig, 1931–1935.* Berkeley; London: University of California Press, 1977.

Kok, Alexander. *A voice in the dark: the philharmonia years.* Ampleforth: Emerson Edition, 2002.

Kopelson, Kevin. *Beethoven's kiss: pianism, perversion, and the mastery of desire.* Stanford, California: Stanford University Press, 1996.

Kostelanetz, Richard, Editor. *Aaron Copland: a reader; selected writings 1923–1972.* New York; London: Routledge, 2003.

Kostelanetz, Richard. *Conversing with Cage.* New York; London: Routledge, 2003.

Kostelanetz, Richard. *On innovative musicians.* New York: Limelight Editions, 1989.

Kostelanetz, Richard, Editor. *Virgil Thomson: a reader ; selected writings, 1924–1984.* New York; London: Routledge, 2002.

Kowalke, Kim H. *Kurt Weill in Europe.* Ann Arbor, Michigan: UMI Research Press, 1979.

Krehbiel, Henry Edward. *The pianoforte and its music.* New York: Cooper Square Publishers, 1971.

Kruseman, Philip, Editor. *Beethoven's own words.* London: Hinrichsen Edition, 1948.

Kurtz, Michael. *Stockhausen: a biography.* London: Faber and Faber, 1992.

Lam, Basil. *Beethoven string quartets.* Seattle: University of Washington Press, 1975.

Lambert, Constant. *Music ho!: a study of music in decline.* London: Faber and Faber, Ltd. 1934.

Landon, H. C. Robbins. *Beethoven: a documentary study.* London: Thames and Hudson, 1970.

Landon, H. C. Robbins. *Beethoven: his life, work and world.* London: Thames and Hudson, 1992.

Landon, H. C. Robbins. *Essays on the Viennese classical style: Gluck, Haydn, Mozart, Beethoven.* London: Barrie & Rockliff The Cresset Press, 1970.

Landon, H. C. Robbins. *Haydn: chronicle and works/Haydn, the late years, 1801–1809.* Bloomington: Indiana University Press, 1977.

Landon, H. C. Robbins. *Haydn: his life and music.* London: Thames and Hudson, 1988.

Landon, H. C. Robbins. *Haydn in England, 1791–1795.* London: Thames and Hudson, 1976.

Landon, H. C. Robbins. Haydn: the years of

'The creation',

1796–800. London: Thames and Hudson, 1977.

Landon, H. C. Robbins. *Mozart: the golden years, 1781–1791.* New York: Schirmer Books, 1989.

Landon, H. C. Robbins. *1791, Mozart's last year.* London: Thames and Hudson, 1988.

Landon, H. C. Robbins *The collected correspondence and London notebooks of Joseph Haydn.* London: Barrie and Rockliff, 1959.

Landon, H. C. Robbins: Editor. *The Mozart companion. London: Faber, 1956.*

Landowska, Wanda. *Music of the past.* London: Geoffrey Bles, 1926.

Lang, Paul Henry. *Musicology and performance.* New Haven: Yale University Press, 1997.

Lang, Paul Henry. *The creative world of Beethoven.* New York: W. W. Norton 1971.

Laurence, Dan H., Editor. *Shaw's music: the complete musical criticism in three volumes.* London: Max Reinhardt, the Bodley Head, 1981.

Lawford-Hinrichsen, Irene. *Music publishing and patronage: C. F. Peters, 1800 to the Holocaust.* Kenton: Edition Press, 2000.

Layton, Robert, Editor. *A guide to the concerto.* Oxford: Oxford University Press, 1996.

Layton, Robert, Editor. *A guide to the symphony.* Oxford: Oxford University Press, 1995.

Lebrecht, Norman. *The maestro myth: great conductors in pursuit of power.* London: Simon & Schuster, 1991.

Lee, Ernest Markham. *The story of the symphony.* London: Scott Publishing Co., 1916.

Leibowitz, Herbert A., Editor. *Musical impressions: selections from Paul Rosenfeld's criticism.* London: G. Allen & Unwin, 1970.

Lenrow, Elbert, Editor and Translator. *The letters of Richard Wagner to Anton Pusinelli.* New York: Vienna House, 1972.

Leonard, Maurice. *Kathleen: the life of Kathleen Ferrier: 1912–1953.* London: Hutchinson, 1988.

Lesure, François and Roger Nichols, Editors. *Debussy, letters.* London: Faber and Faber, 1987.

Letellier, Robert Ignatius, Editor and Translator. *The diaries of Giacomo Meyerbeer.* Madison: Fairleigh Dickinson University Press; London: Associated University Presses, 4 Vols., 1999–2004.

Levas, Santeri. *Sibelius: a personal portrait.* London: J. M. Dent, 1972.

Levy, Alan Howard. *Edward MacDowell, an American master.* Lanham, Md. & London: Scarecrow Press, 1998.

Levy, David Benjamin. *Beethoven: the Ninth Symphony.* New Haven, Connecticut; London: Yale University Press, 2003.

Leyda, Jay and Sergi Bertensson. *The Musorgsky reader: a life of Modeste Petrovich Musorgsky in letters and documents.* New York: W.W. Norton, 1947.

Lewis, Thomas P., Editor. *Raymond Leppard on music: an anthology of critical and personal writings.* White Plains, N.Y.: Pro/Am Music Resources, 1993.

Liébert, Georges. *Nietzsche and music.* Chicago: University of Chicago Press, 2004.

Liszt, Franz. *An artist's journey: lettres d'un bachelier ès musique, 1835–1841.* Chicago: University of Chicago Press, 1989.

Litzmann, Berthold, Editor. *Clara Schumann: an artist's life, based on material found in diaries and letters.* London: Macmillan; Leipzig: Breitkopf & Härtel, 2 Vols. 1913.

Litzmann, Berthold, Editor. *Letters of Clara Schumann and Johannes Brahms, 1853–1896.* New York, Vienna House. 2 Vols. 1971.

Lloyd, Stephen. *William Walton: muse of fire.* Woodbridge, Suffolk: The Boydell Press, 2001.

Locke, Ralph P. and Cyrilla Barr, Editors. *Cultivating music in America: women patrons and activists since 1860.* Berkeley: University of California Press, 1997.

Lockspeiser, Edward. *Debussy: his life and mind.* London: Cassell. 2 Vols. 1962–1965.

Lockspeiser, Edward. *The literary clef: an anthology of letters and writings by French composers.* London: J. Calder. 1958.

Lockwood, Lewis, Editor. *Beethoven essays: studies in honor of Elliot Forbes.* Cambridge, Massachusetts: Harvard University Department of Music: Distributed by Harvard University Press, 1984.

Lockwood, Lewis and Mark Kroll, Editors. *The Beethoven violin sonatas: history, criticism, performance.* Urbana: University of Illinois Press, 2004.

Loft, Abram. *Violin and keyboard: the duo repertoire.* New York: Grossman Publishers. 2 Vols. 1973.

Longyear, Rey Morgan. *Nineteenth-century romanticism in music.* Englewood Cliffs: Prentice-Hall, 1969.

Lowe, C. Egerton. *Beethoven's pianoforte sonatas: hints on their rendering, form, etc., with appendices on definition of sonata, music forms, ornaments, pianoforte pedals, and how to discover keys.* London: Novello, 1929.

Macdonald, Hugh, Editor. *Berlioz: Selected letters.* London: Faber and Faber, 1995.

Macdonald, Malcolm, Editor. *Havergal Brian on music: selections from his journalism: Volume One, British music.* London:

Toccata Press, 1986.

MacDonald, Malcolm. *Varèse: astronomer in sound.* London: Kahn & Averill, 2003.

MacDowell, Edward. *Critical and historical essays: lectures delivered at Columbia University.* Edited by W. J. Baltzell. London: Elkin; Boston: A.P. Schmidt, 1912.

MacFarren, Walter. Memories: an autobiography. London: Walter Scott Publishing Co.,1905.

Mackenzie, Alexander Campbell. *A musician's narrative.* London: Cassell and company, Ltd, 1927.

McCarthy, Margaret William, Editor. *More letters of Amy Fay: the American years, 1879–1916.* Detroit: Information Coordinators, 1986.

McClary, Susan. *Feminine endings: music, gender, and sexuality.* Minneapolis: University of Minnesota Press, 1991.

McClatchie, Stephen, Editor and Translator. *The Mahler family letters.* Oxford: Oxford University Press, 2006.

McVeigh, Simon. *Concert life in London from Mozart to Haydn.* Cambridge: Cambridge University Press, 1993.

Mahler, Alma. *Gustav Mahler: memories and letters.* Enlarged edition revised and edited and with and introduction by Donald Mitchell. London: John Murray, 1968.

Mai, François Martin. *Diagnosing genius: the life and death of Beethoven.* Montreal; London: McGill-Queen's University Press, 2007.

Del Mar, Norman. *Orchestral variations: confusion and error in the orchestral repertoire.* London: Eulenburg, 1981.

Del Mar, Norman. *Richard Strauss: a critical commentary on his life and works.* London: Barrie & Jenkins. 3 Vols. 1978.

(La) Mara [pseudonym]. *Letters of Franz Liszt.* London: H. Grevel & Co., 2 Vols. 1894.

Marek, George Richard. *Puccini.* London: Cassell & Co., 1952.

Marek, George Richard. *Toscanini.* London: Vision, 1976.

(De) Marliave, Joseph. *Beethoven's quartets.* New York: Dover Publications (reprint), 1961.

Martin, George Whitney. *Verdi: his music, life and times.* London: Macmillan, 1965.

Martner, Knud, Editor. *Selected letters of Gustav Mahler.* London; Boston: Faber and Faber, 1979.

Martyn, Barrie. *Nicolas Medtner: his life and music.* Aldershot: Scolar Press, 1995.

Martyn, Barrie. *Rachmaninoff: composer, pianist, conductor.* Aldershot: Scolar, 1990.

Massenet, Jules. *My recollections.* Westport, Connecticut: Greenwood Press.1970.

Matheopoulos, Helena. *Maestro: encounters with conductors of today.* London: Hutchinson, 1982.

Matthews, Denis. *Beethoven.* London: J. M. Dent, 1985.

Matthews, Denis. *Beethoven piano sonatas.* London: British Broadcasting Corporation, 1967.

Matthews, Dennis. *In pursuit of music.* London: Victor Gollancz Ltd., 1968.

Matthews, Denis. *Keyboard music.* Newton Abbot: London David

Mellers, Wilfrid Howard. *Caliban reborn: renewal in twentieth-century music.* London: Victor Gollancz, 1967.

Mellers, Wilfrid Howard. *The sonata principle (from c. 1750).* London: Rockliff, 1957.

Mendelssohn Bartholdy. *Letters from Italy and Switzerland.* London: Longman, Green, Longman, and Roberts, 1862.

Mendelssohn Bartholdy, Paul. *Letters of Felix Mendelssohn Bartholdy, from 1833 to 1847.* London: Longman, Green, Longman, Roberts, & Green, 1864.

Menuhin, Yehudi and Curtis W. Davis. *The music of man.* London: Macdonald and Jane's, 1979.

Menuhin, Yehudi. *Theme and variations.* London: Heinemann Educational Books Ltd., 1972.

Menuhin, Yehudi. *Unfinished journey.* London: Macdonald and Jane's, 1977.

Messian, Olivier. *Music and color: conversations with Claude Samuel.* Portland, Oregon: Amadeus, 1994.

Miall, Antony. *Musical bumps.* London: J.M. Dent & Sons Ltd, 1981.

Michotte, Edmond. *Richard Wagner's visit to Rossini (Paris 1860): and, An evening at Rossini's in Beau-Sejour (Passy), 1858.* Chicago; London: University of Chicago Press, 1982.

Mies, Paul. *Beethoven's sketches: an analysis of his style based on a study of his sketchbooks.* New York: Johnson Reprint, 1969.

Milhaud, Darius. *My happy life.* London: Boyars, 1995.

Miller, Mina. *The Nielsen companion.* London: Faber and Faber, 1994.

Milsom, David. *Theory and practice in late nineteenth-century violin performance: an examination of style in performance, 1850–1900.* Aldershot: Ashgate, 2003.

Mitchell, Donald, Editor. *Letters from a life: the selected letters and diaries of Benjamin Britten 1913–1976.* London: Faber and Faber. 3 Vols., 1991.

Mitchell, Donald and Hans Keller, Editors. *Music survey: new series 1949–1952.* London: Faber Music in association with Faber & Faber, 1981.

Mitchell, Jon C. *A comprehensive biography of composer Gustav Holst, with correspondence and diary excerpts: including his American years.* Lewiston, New York: Edwin Mellen Press, 2001.

Moldenhauer, Hans. *Anton von Webern: a chronicle of his life and work.* London: Victor Gollancz, 1978.

Monrad-Johansen. Edvard Grieg. New York: Tudor Publishing Co., 1945.

Moore, Gerald. *Am I too loud?: memoirs of an accompanist.* London: Hamish Hamilton, 1962.

Moore, Gerald. *Farewell recital: further memoirs.* Harmondsworth: Penguin Books, 1979.

Moore, Gerald. *Furthermoore: interludes in an accompanist's life.* London: Hamish Hamilton, 1983.

Moore, Jerrold Northrop. *Edward Elgar: a creative life.* Oxford: Oxford University Press, 1984.

Moore, Jerrold Northrop. *Elgar, Edward. The windflower letters: correspondence with Alice Caroline Stuart Wortley and her family*. Oxford: Clarendon Press; New York: Oxford University Press, 1989.

Moore, Jerrold Northrop. *Elgar, Edward. Edward Elgar: letters of a lifetime*. Oxford: Clarendon Press; New York: Oxford University Press, 1990.

Moore, Jerrold Northrop. *Elgar, Edward. Elgar and his publishers: letters of a creative life*. Oxford: Clarendon, 1987.

Moreux, Serge. *Béla Bartók*. London: Harvill Press, 1953.

Morgan, Kenneth. *Fritz Reiner, maestro and martinet*. Urbana: University of Illinois Press, 2005.

Cone, Edward T., Editor. *Music, a view from Delft: selected essays*. Chicago: University of Chicago Press, 1989.

Morgan, Robert P. *Twentieth-century music: a history of musical style in modern Europe and America*. New York: Norton, 1991.

Morgenstern, Sam., Editor. *Composers on music: an anthology of composers' writings*. London: Faber & Faber, 1956.

Morrow, Mary Sue. *Concert life in Haydn's Vienna: aspects of a developing musical and social institution*. Stuyvesant, New York: Pendragon Press, 1989.

Moscheles, Felix, Editor and Translator. *Letters from Felix Mendelssohn-Bartholdy to Ignaz and Charlotte Moscheles*. London: Trübner and Co., 1888.

Mudge, Richard B., Translator. *Glinka, Mikhail Ivanovich: Memoirs*. Norman: University of Oklahoma Press, 1963.

Munch, Charles. *I am a conductor*. New York: Oxford University Press, 1955.

Mundy, Simon. *Bernard Haitink: a working life*. London: Robson Books, 1987.

Musgrave, Michael. *The musical life of the Crystal Palace*. Cambridge: Cambridge University Press, 1995.

Music & Letters. *Beethoven: special number*. London: Music & Letters, 1927.

Musical Times. *Special Issue*. John A. Fuller-Maitland London: Vol. VIII, No. 2, 1927.

Myers, Rollo H., Editor. *Twentieth-century music*. London: Calder and Boyars, 1960.

National Gallery (Great Britain). *Music performed at the National Gallery concerts, 10th October 1939 to 10th April 1946*. London: Privately printed, 1948.

Nattiez, Jean-Jacques, Editor. *Orientations: collected writings — Pierre Boulez*. London: Faber and Faber, 1986.

Nauhaus, Gerd, Editor. *The marriage diaries of Robert & Clara Schumann*. London: Robson Books, 1994.

Nectoux, Jean Michel. *Gabriel Fauré: a musical life*. Translated by Roger Nichols. Cambridge: Cambridge University Press, 1991.

Nettl, Paul. *Beethoven handbook*. Westport, Connecticut: Greenwood Press, 1975.

Neumayr, Anton. *Music and medicine*. Bloomington, Illinois: Medi-Ed Press, 1994–1997

Newbould, Brian. *Schubert and the symphony: a new perspective*.

Surbiton: Toccata Press, 1992.

Newlin, Dika. *Schoenberg remembered: diaries and recollections (1938–76)*. New York: Pendragon Press, 1980.

Newman, Ernest. From the world of music: essays from 'The Sunday Times'. London: J. Calder, 1956.

Newman, Ernest. Hugo Wolf. New York: Dover Publications, 1966.

Newman, Ernest, Annotated and Translated. *Memoirs of Hector Berlioz from 1803 to 1865, comprising his travels in Germany, Italy, Russia, and England*. New York: Knopf, 1932.

Newman, Ernest. More essays from the world of music: essays from the 'Sunday Times'. London: John Calder, 1958.

Newman, Ernest. *Musical studies*. London; New York: John Lane, 1910.

Newman, Ernest. *Testament of music: essays and papers*. London: Putnam, 1962.

Newman, Richard. *Alma Rosé: Vienna to Auschwitz*. Portland, Oregon: Amadeus Press, 2000.

Newman, William S. *The sonata in the classic era*. Chapel Hill: University of North Carolina Press 1963.

Newman, William S. *The sonata in the Classic era*. New York; London: W.W. Norton, 1983.

Newmarch, Rosa Harriet. *Henry J. Wood*. London & New York: John Lane, 1904.

Nicholas, Jeremy. *Godowsky: the pianists' pianist; a biography of Leopold Godowsky*. Hexham: Appian Publications & Recordings, 1989.

Nichols, Roger. *Debussy remembered*. London: Faber and Faber, 1992.

Nichols, Roger. *Mendelssohn remembered*. London: Faber and Faber, 1997.

Nichols, Roger. *Ravel remembered*. London: Faber and Faber, 1987.

Niecks, Frederick. *Robert Schumann*. London: J. M. Dent, 1925.

Nielsen, Carl. *Living music*. Copenhagen, Wilhelm Hansen, 1968.

Nielsen, Carl. *My childhood*. Copenhagen, Wilhelm Hansen, 1972.

Nikolska, Irina. *Conversations with Witold Lutoslawski, (1987–92)*. Stockholm: Melos, 1994.

Nohl, Ludwig. *Beethoven depicted by his contemporaries*. London: Reeves, 1880.

De Nora, Tia. *Beethoven and the construction of genius: musical politics in Vienna, 1792–1803*. Berkeley: University of California Press, 1997.

Norton, Spencer, Editor and Translator. *Music in my time: the memoirs of Alfredo Casella*. Norman: University of Oklahoma Press, 1955.

Nottebohm, Gustav. *Two Beethoven sketchbooks: a description with musical extracts*. London: Gollancz, 1979.

Oakeley, Edward Murray. *The life of Sir Herbert Stanley Oakeley*. London: George Allen, 1904.

Lucas, Brenda and Michael Kerr. *Virtuoso: the story of John Ogdon*. London: H. Hamilton, 1981.

Oliver, Michael, Editor. *Settling the score: a journey through the music of the twentieth century*. London: Faber and Faber, 1999.

Olleson, Philip. *Samuel Wesley: the man and his music*. Wood-

bridge: Boydell Press, 2003.
Olleson, Philip, Editor. *The letters of Samuel Wesley: professional and social correspondence, 1797–1837.* Oxford; New York: Oxford University Press, 2001.
Olmstead, Andrea. *Conversations with Roger Sessions.* Boston: Northeastern University Press, 1987.
Orenstein, Arbie, Editor. *A Ravel reader: correspondence, articles, interviews.* New York: Columbia University Press, 1990.
Orenstein, Arbie. *Ravel: man and musician.* New York: Columbia University Press, 1975.
Orledge, Robert. *Charles Koechlin (1867–1950): his life and works.* New York: Harwood Academic Publishers, 1989.
Orledge, Robert. *Gabriel Fauré.* London: Eulenburg Books, 1979.
Orledge, Robert. *Satie remembered.* London: Faber and Faber, 1995.
Orledge, Robert. *Satie the composer.* Cambridge: Cambridge University Press, 1990.
Orlova, Alexandra. *Glinka's life in music: a chronicle.* Ann Arbor: UMI Research Press, 1988.
Orlova, Alexandra. *Musorgsky's days and works: a biography in documents.* Ann Arbor: UMI Research Press, 1983.
Orlova, Alexandra. *Tchaikovsky: a self-portrait.* Oxford: Oxford University Press, 1990.
Osborne, Charles, Editor and Translator. *Letters of Giuseppe Verdi.* London: Victor Gollancz, 1971.
Osmond-Smith David, Editor and Translator. *Luciano Berio: Two interviews with Rossana Dalmonte and Bálint András Varga.* New York; London: Boyars, 1985.
Ouellette, Fernand. *Edgard Varèse.* London: Calder & Boyars, 1973.
Paderewski, Ignacy Jan and Mary Lawton. *The Paderewski memoirs.* London: Collins, 1939.
Page, Tim: Editor. *The Glenn Gould reader.* London: Faber and Faber, 1987.
Page, Tim. *Music from the road: views and reviews, 1978–1992.* New York; Oxford: Oxford University Press, 1992.
Page, Tim and Vanessa Weeks, Editors. *Selected letters of Virgil Thomson.* New York: Summit Books, 1988.
Page, Tim. *Tim Page on music: views and reviews.* Portland, Oregon: Amadeus Press, 2002.
Palmer, Christopher. *Herbert Howells, (1892–1983): a celebration.* London: Thames, 1996.
Palmer, Christopher, Editor. *Sergei Prokofiev: Soviet diary 1927 and other writings.* London: Faber and Faber, 1991.
Palmer, Fiona M. *Domenico Dragonetti in England (1794–1846): the career of a double bass virtuoso.* Oxford: Clarendon, 1997.
Palmieri, Robert, Editor. *Encyclopedia of the piano.* New York: Garland, 1996.
Panufnik, Andrzej. *Composing myself.* London: Methuen, 1987.
Parsons, James, Editor. *The Cambridge companion to the Lied.* Cambridge: Cambridge University Press, 2004.
Paynter, John, Editor. *Between old worlds and new: occasional writings on music by Wilfrid Mellers.* London: Cygnus Arts, 1997.
Pestelli, Giorgio. *The age of Mozart*

and Beethoven. Cambridge: Cambridge University Press, 1984.

Peyser, Joan. *Bernstein: a biography: revised & updated.* New York: Billboard Books, 1998.

Phillips-Matz, Mary Jane. *Verdi: a biography.* Oxford: Oxford University Press, 1993.

Piggott, Patrick. *The life and music of John Field, 1782–1837: creator of the nocturne.* London: Faber and Faber, 1973.

Plantinga, Leon. *Beethoven's concertos: history, style, performance.* New York: Norton, 1999.

Plantinga, Leon. *Clementi: his life and music.* London: Oxford University Press, 1977.

Plantinga, Leon. *Romantic music: a history of musical style in nineteenth-century Europe.* New York; London: Norton, 1984.

Plaskin, Glenn. *Horowitz: a biography of Vladimir Horowitz.* London: Macdonald, 1983.

Pleasants, Henry, Editor and Translator. *Hanslick, Eduard: Music criticisms, 1846–99.* Baltimore: Penguin Books, 1963.

Pleasants, Henry, Editor and Translator. *Hanslick's music criticisms.* New York: Dover Publications, 1988.

Pleasants, Henry, Editor and Translator. *The music criticism of Hugo Wolf.* New York: Holmes & Meier Publishers, 1978.

Pleasants, Henry, Editor and Translator. *The musical journeys of Louis Spohr.* Norman: University of Oklahoma Press, 1961.

Pollack, Howard. *Aaron Copland: the life and work of an uncommon man.* New York: Henry Holt, 1999.

Poulenc, Francis. *My friends and myself.* London: Dennis Dobson, 1978.

Powell, Richard, Mrs. *Edward Elgar: memories of a variation.* Aldershot, Hants, England: Scolar Press; Brookfield, Vermont, USA: Ashgate Publishing. Co., 1994.

Poznansky, Alexander, Editor. *Tchaikovsky through others' eyes.* Bloomington: Indiana University Press, 1999.

Praeger, Ferdinand. *Wagner as I knew him.* London; New York: Longmans, Green, 1892.

Previn, Andre. *Antony Hopkins. Music face to face.* London, Hamish Hamilton, 1971.

Prieberg, Fred K. *Trial of strength: Wilhelm Furtwängler and the Third Reich.* London: Quartet, 1991.

Procter-Gregg, Humphrey. *Beecham remembered.* London: Duckworth, 1976.

Prokofiev, Sergey. *Prokofiev by Prokofiev: a composer's memoir.* London: Macdonald and Jane's, 1979.

Rachmaninoff, Sergei. *Rachmaninoff's recollections told to Oskar von Riesemann.* London: George Allen & Unwin, 1934.

Radcliffe, Philip. *Beethoven's string quartets.* Cambridge: Cambridge University Press, 1978.

Radcliffe, Philip. *Piano Music in: The Age of Beethoven, The New Oxford History of Music, Vol. VIII.* Gerald Abraham, (Editor), 1988, p. 340.

Ratner, Leonard G. *Romantic music: sound and syntax.* New York: Schirmer Books, 1992.

Raynor, Henry. *A social history of*

music: from the middle ages to Beethoven. London: Barrie & Jenkins, 1972.

Rees, Brian. *Camille Saint-Saëns: a life*. London: Chatto & Windus, 1999.

Reich, Willi, Editor. *Anton Webern: The path to the new music*. London; Bryn Mawr: Theodore Presser in association with Universal Edition, 1963.

Reid, Charles. *John Barbirolli: a biography*. London, Hamish Hamilton, 1971.

Reid, Charles. *Malcolm Sargent: a biography*. London: Hamilton, 1968.

Rennert, Jonathan. *William Crotch (1775–1847): composer, artist, teacher*. Lavenham: Terence Dalton, 1975.

Rice, John A. *Antonio Salieri and Viennese Opera*. Chicago, Illinois: University of Chicago Press, 1998.

Rice, John A. *Empress Marie Therese and music at the Viennese court, 1792–1807*. Cambridge: Cambridge University Press, 2003.

Richards, Fiona. *The Music of John Ireland*. Aldershot: Ashgate, 2000.

Rigby, Charles. *Sir Charles Hallé: a portrait for today*. Manchester: Dolphin Press, 1952.

Ringer, Alexander, Editor. *The early Romantic era: between Revolutions; 1789 and 1848*. Basingstoke: Macmillan, 1990.

Roberts, John P.L. and Ghyslaine Guertin, Editors. *Glenn Gould: Selected letters*. Toronto; Oxford: Oxford University Press, 1992.

Robertson, Alec. *More than music*. London: Collins, 1961.

Robinson, Harlow, Editor and Translator. *Selected letters of Sergei Prokofiev*. Boston: Northeastern University Press, 1998.

Robinson, Harlow. *Sergei Prokofiev: a biography*. London: Hale, 1987.

Robinson, Paul A. *Ludwig van Beethoven, Fidelio*. Cambridge: Cambridge University Press, 1996.

Robinson, Suzanne, Editor. *Michael Tippett: music and literature*. Aldershot: Ashgate, 2002.

Rochberg, George. *The aesthetics of survival: a composer's view of twentieth-century music*. Ann Arbor, Michigan: University of Michigan Press, 2004.

Rodmell, Paul. *Charles Villiers Stanford*. Aldershot: Ashgate, 2002.

Roeder, Michael Thomas. *A history of the concerto*. Portland, Oregon: Amadeus Press, 1994.

Rohr, Deborah Adams. *The careers of British musicians, 1750–1850: a profession of artisans*. Cambridge: Cambridge University Press, 2001.

Rolland, Romain. *Goethe and Beethoven*. New York; London: Blom, 1968.

Rolland, Romain. *Beethoven and Handel*. London: Waverley Book Co., 1917.

Rolland, Romain. *Beethoven the creator*. Garden City, New York: Garden City Pub., 1937.

Roscow, Gregory, Editor. *Bliss on music: selected writings of Arthur Bliss, 1920–1975*. Oxford: Oxford University Press, 1991.

Rosen, Charles. *Beethoven's piano sonatas: a short companion*. New

Haven, Connecticut: London: Yale University Press, 2002.

Rosen, Charles. *Critical entertainments: music old and new.* Cambridge, Massachusetts; London: Harvard University Press, 2000.

Rosen, Charles. *The classical style: Haydn, Mozart, Beethoven.* London: Faber and Faber, 1976.

Rosen, Charles. *The romantic generation.* Cambridge, Massachusetts: Harvard University Press, 1995.

Rosenthal, Albi. *Obiter scripta: essays, lectures, articles, interviews and reviews on music, and other subjects.* Oxford: Offox Press; Lanham: Scarecrow Press, 2000.

Rostal, Max. *Beethoven: the sonatas for piano and violin; thoughts on their interpretation.* London: Toccata Press, 1985.

Rostropovich, Mstislav and Galina Vishnevskaya. *Russia, music, and liberty.* Portland, Oregan: Amadeus Press, 1995.

Rubinstein, Arthur. *My many years.* London: Jonathan Cape, 1980.

Rubinstein, Arthur. *My young years.* London: Jonathan Cape, 1973.

Rumph, Stephen C. *Beethoven after Napoleon: political romanticism in the late works.* Berkeley; London: University of California Press, 2004.

Rye, Matthew Rye. *Notes to the BBC Radio Three Beethoven Experience, Friday 10 June 2005,* www.bbc.co.uk/radio3/Beethoven.

Sachs, Harvey. *Toscanini.* London: Weidenfeld and Nicholson, 1978.

Sachs, Joel. *Kapellmeister Hummel in England and France.* Detroit: Information Coordinators, 1977.

Saffle, Michael, Editor. *Liszt and his world: proceedings of the International Liszt Conference held at Virginia Polytechnic Institute and State University, 20–23 May 1993.* Stuyvesant, New York: Pendragon Press, 1998.

Safránek, Milos. *Bohuslav Martinu, his life and works.* London: Allan Wingate, 1962.

Saint-Saëns, Camille. *Outspoken essays on music.* Westport, Connecticut: Greenwood Press, 1970.

Saussine, Renée de. *Paganini.* Westport, Connecticut: Greenwood Press, 1976.

Sayers, W. C. Berwick. *Samuel Coleridge-Taylor, musician: his life and letters.* London; New York: Cassell and Co., 1915.

Schaarwächter, Jürgen. *HB: aspects of Havergal Brian.* Aldershot: Ashgate, 1997.

Schafer, R. Murray. *E.T.A. Hoffmann and music.* Toronto: University of Toronto Press, 1975.

Schafer, R. Murray, Editor. *Ezra Pound and music: the complete criticism.* London: Faber and Faber, 1978.

Schat, Peter. *The tone clock.* Chur, Switzerland; Langhorne, Pa.: Harwood Academic Publishers, 1993.

Schenk, Erich. *Mozart and his times.* Edited and Translated by Richard and Clara Winstin. London: Secker & Warburg, 1960.

Schindler, Anton Felix. *Beethoven as I knew him.* Edited by Donald W. MacArdle and Translated by Constance S. Jolly from the German edition of 1860

London: Faber and Faber, 1966.

Schlosser, Johann. *Beethoven: the first biography, 1827*. Edited by Barry Cooper. Portland, Oregon: Amadeus Press, 1996.

Schnabel, Artur. *My life and music*. London: Longmans, 1961.

Schnittke, Alfred. *A Schnittke reader*. Bloomington: Indiana University Press, 2002.

Scholes, Percy Alfred. *Crotchets: a few short musical notes*. London: John Lane, 1924.

Schonberg, Harold C. *The great pianists*. London: Victor Gollancz, 1964.

Schrade, Leo. *Beethoven in France: the growth of an idea*. New Haven; London: Yale University Press, H. Milford, Oxford University Press, 1942.

Schrade, Leo. *Tragedy in the art of music*. Cambridge, Massachusetts: Harvard University Press, 1964.

Schuh, Willi. *Richard Strauss: a chronicle of the early years 1864–1898*. Cambridge: Cambridge University Press, 1982.

Schuh, Willi, Editor. *Richard Strauss: Recollections and reflections*. London; New York: Boosey & Hawkes, 1953.

Schuller, Gunther. *Musings: the musical worlds of Gunther Schuller*. New York: Oxford University Press, 1986.

Schumann, Robert. *Music and musicians: essays and criticisms*. London: William Reeves, 1877.

Schuttenhelm, Editor. *Selected letters of Michael Tippett*. London: Faber and Faber, 2005.

Schwartz, Elliott. *Music since 1945: issues, materials, and literature*. New York: Schirmer Books, 1993.

Scott, Marion M. *Beethoven: (The master musicians)*. London: Dent, 1940.

Scott-Sutherland, Colin. *Arnold Bax*. London: J. M. Dent, 1973.

Searle, Muriel V. *John Ireland: the man and his music*. Tunbridge Wells: Midas Books, 1979.

Secrest, Meryle. *Leonard Bernstein: a life*. London: Bloomsbury, 1995.

Seeger, Charles. *Studies in musicology II, 1929–1979*. Edited by Anne M. Pescatello. Berkeley; London: University of California Press, 1994.

Selden-Goth, Gisela, Editor. *Felix Mendelssohn: letters*. London: Paul Elek Publishers Ltd, 1946.

Senner, Wayne M., Robin Wallace and William Meredith, Editors. *The critical reception of Beethoven's compositions by his German contemporaries*. Lincoln: University of Nebraska Press, in association with the American Beethoven Society and the Ira F. Brilliant Center for Beethoven Studies, San José State University, 1999.

Seroff, Victor I. *Rachmaninoff*. London: Cassell & Company, 1951.

Sessions, Roger. *Questions about music*. Cambridge, Massachusetts: Harvard University Press, 1970.

Sessions, Roger. *The musical experience of composer, performer, listener*. New York: Atheneum, 1966, 1950.

Seyfried, Ignaz von. *Louis van Beethoven's Studies in thoroughbass, counterpoint and the art of scientific composition*. Leipzig;

New-York: Schuberth and Company, 1853.

Sharma, Bhesham R. *Music and culture in the age of mechanical reproduction.* New York: Peter Lang, 2000.

Shaw, Bernard. *How to become a musical critic.* London: R. Hart Davis, 1960.

Shaw, Bernard. *London music in 1888–89 as heard by Corno di Bassetto (later known as Bernard Shaw): with some further autobiographical particulars.* London: Constable and Company, 1937.

Shaw, Bernard. *Music in London, 1890–1894.* London: Constable and Company Limited, 3 Vols., 1932.

Shedlock, John South. *Beethoven's pianoforte sonatas: the origin and respective values of various readings.* London: Augener Ltd., 1918.

Shedlock, John South. *The pianoforte sonata: its origin and development.* London: Methuen, 1895.

Shepherd, Arthur. *The string quartets of Ludwig van Beethoven.* Cleveland: H. Carr, The Printing Press, 1935.

Sheppard, Leslie and Herbert R. Axelrod. *Paganini: containing a portfolio of drawings by Vido Polikarpus.* Neptune City, New Jersey: Paganiniana Publications, 1979.

Short, Michael. *Gustav Holst: the man and his music.* Oxford: Oxford University Press, 1990.

Shostakovich, Dmitry. *Dmitry Shostakovich: about himself and his times.* Moscow: Progress Publishers, 1981.

Simpson, John Palgrave. *Carl Maria von Weber: the life of an artist, from the German of his son Baron, Max Maria von Weber.* London: Chapman and Hall, 1865.

Simpson, Robert. *Beethoven symphonies.* London: British Broadcasting Corporation, 1970.

Sipe, Thomas. *Beethoven: Eroica symphony.* Cambridge: Cambridge University Press, 1998.

Sitwell, Sacheverell. *Mozart.* Edinburgh: Peter Davies Limited, 1932.

Skelton, Geoffrey. *Paul Hindemith: the man behind the music; a biography.* London: Victor Gollancz, 1975.

Smallman, Basil. *The piano trio: its history, technique, and repertoire.* Oxford: Clarendon Press; Oxford; New York: Oxford University Press, 1990.

Smidak, Emil. *Isaak-Ignaz Moscheles: the life of the composer and his encounters with Beethoven, Liszt, Chopin, and Mendelssohn.* Aldershot, Hampshire, England: Scolar Press; Brookfield, Vermont, USA: Gower Publishing Co., 1989.

Smith, Barry. *Peter Warlock: the life of Philip Heseltine.* Oxford: Oxford University Press, 1994.

Smith, Joan Allen. *Schoenberg and his circle: a Viennese portrait.* New York: Schirmer Books, London: Collier Macmillan, 1986.

Smith, Richard Langham, Editor. *Debussy on music: the critical writings of the great French composer Claude Debussy.* London: Secker & Warburg, 1977.

Smith, Ronald. *Alkan.* London: Kahn and Averill, 1976.

Snowman, Daniel. *The Amadeus Quartet: the men and the music.* London: Robson Books, 1981.

Solomon, Maynard. *Beethoven.* New York: Schirmer, 1977.

Solomon, Maynard. *Beethoven essays.* Cambridge, Massachusetts; London: Harvard University Press, 1988.

Solomon, Maynard. *Late Beethoven: music, thought, imagination.* Berkeley; London: University of California Press, 2003.

Solomon, Maynard. *Mozart: a life.* London: Hutchinson, 1995.

Sonneck, Oscar George Theodore. *Beethoven: impressions of contemporaries.* London: Oxford University Press, 1927.

Spalding, Albert. *Rise to follow: an autobiography.* London: Frederick Muller Ltd., 1946.

Spohr, Louis. *Louis Spohr's autobiography.* London: Longman, Green, Longman, Roberts, & Green, 1865.

Stafford, William. *Mozart myths: a critical reassessment.* Stanford, California: Stanford University Press, 1991.

Stanford, Charles Villiers. *Interludes: records and reflections.* London: John Murray, 1922.

Stanley, Glenn, Editor. *The Cambridge companion to Beethoven.* Cambridge; New York: Cambridge University Press, 2000

Stedman, Preston. *The symphony.* Englewood Cliffs, New Jersey; London: Prentice-Hall, 1979.

Stedron, Bohumír, Editor and Translator. *Leos Janácek: letters and reminiscences.* Prague: Artia, 1955.

Stein, Erwin, Editor. *Arnold Schoenberg: letters.* London: Faber and Faber, 1964.

Stein, Erwin. *Orpheus in new guises.* London: Rockliff, 1953.

Stein, Jack Madison. *Poem and music in the German lied from Gluck to Hugo Wolf.* Cambridge, Massachusetts: Harvard University Press, 1971.

Stein, Leonard, Editor. *Style and idea: selected writings of Arnold Schoenberg.* London: Faber and Faber, 1975.

Steinberg, Michael P. *Listening to reason: culture, subjectivity, and nineteenth-century music.* Princeton, New Jersey: Princeton University Press, 2004.

Steinberg, Michael. *The concerto: a listener's guide.* New York: Oxford University Press, 1998.

Steinberg, Michael. *The symphony: a listener's guide.* Oxford; New York: Oxford University Press, 1995.

Sternfeld, Frederick William. *Goethe and music: a list of parodies and Goethe's relationship to music; a list of references.* New York: Da Capo Press, 1979.

Stivender, David. *Mascagni: an autobiography compiled, edited and translated from original sources.* New York: Pro/Am Music Resources; London: Kahn & Averill, 1988.

Stone, Else and Kurt Stone, Editors. *The writings of Elliott Carter: an American composer looks at modern music.* Bloomington: Indiana University Press, 1977.

Stowell, Robin. *Beethoven: violin concerto.* Cambridge: Cambridge University Press, 1998.

Stowell, Robin: Editor. *The Cambridge companion to the cello.* Cambridge: Cambridge University Press, 1999.

Stowell, Robin: Editor. *The Cambridge companion to the string quartet.* Cambridge: Cambridge University Press, 2003.

Stratton, Stephen Samuel. *Mendelssohn.* London: J.M. Dent & Co.; New York: E.P. Dutton & Co., 1901.

Straus, Joseph N. *Remaking the past: musical modernism and the influence of the tonal tradition.* Cambridge, Massachusetts: Harvard University Press, 1990.

Stravinsky, Igor. *An autobiography.* London: Calder and Boyars, 1975.

Stravinsky, Igor. *Themes and conclusions.* London: Faber and Faber, 1972.

Stravinsky, Igor and Robert Craft. *Conversations with Igor Stravinsky.* London: Faber and Faber, 1959.

Stravinsky, Igor and Robert Craft. *Dialogues and a diary.* London: Faber and Faber 1968.

Stravinsky, Igor and Robert Craft. *Memories and commentaries.* London: Faber and Faber, 2002.

Strunk, Oliver. *Source readings in music history, 4: The Classic era.* London: Faber and Faber 1981.

Sullivan, Blair, Editor. *The echo of music: essays in honor of Marie Louise Göllner.* Warren, Michigan: Harmonie Park Press, 2004.

Sullivan, Jack, Editor. *Words on music: from Addison to Barzun.* Athens: Ohio University Press, 1990.

Symonette, Lys and Kim H. Kowalke, Editors and Translators. *Speak low (when you speak love): the letters of Kurt Weill and Lotte Lenya.* London: Hamish Hamilton, 1996.

Swalin, Benjamin F. *The violin concerto: a study in German romanticism.* New York, Da Capo Press, 1973.

Szigeti, Joseph. *With strings attached: reminiscences and reflections.* London: Cassell & Co. Ltd, 1949.

Tanner, Michael, Editor. *Notebooks, 1924–1954: Wilhelm Furtwängler.* London: Quartet Books, 1989.

Taylor, Robert, Editor. *Furtwängler on music: essays and addresses.* Aldershot: Scolar, 1991.

Taylor, Ronald. *Kurt Weill: composer in a divided world.* London: Simon & Schuster, 1991.

Tchaikovsky, Peter Ilich. *Letters to his family: an autobiography.* Translated by Galina von Meck. London: Dennis Dobson, 1981.

Tertis, Lionel. My viola and I: a complete autobiography; with,

'Beauty of tone in string playing',

and other essays. London: Paul Elek, 1974.

Thayer, Alexander Wheelock. *Salieri: rival of Mozart.* Edited by Theodore Albrecht. Kansas City, Missouri: Philharmonia of Greater Kansas City, 1989.

Thomas, Michael Tilson. *Viva voce: conversations with Edward Seckerson.* London: Faber and Faber 1994.

Thomson, Andrew. *Vincent d'Indy and his world.* Oxford: Clarendon Press, 1996.

Thomson, Virgil. *The musical scene.* New York: Greenwood Press, 1968.

Thomson, Virgil. *Virgil Thomson.* London: Weidenfeld & Nicolson, 1967.

Tillard, Françoise. *Fanny Mendelssohn.* Amadeus Press: Portland, 1996.

Tilmouth, Michael, Editor. *Donald Francis Tovey: The classics of music: talks, essays, and other writings previously uncollected.* Oxford: Oxford University Press, 2001

Tippett, Michael. *Moving into Aquarius.* London: Routledge and Kegan Paul, 1959.

Tippett, Michael. *Those twentieth century blues: an autobiography.* London: Hutchinson, 1991.

Todd, R. Larry, Editor. *Nineteenth-century piano music.* New York; London: Routledge, 2004.

Todd, R. Larry, Editor. *Schumann and his world.* Princeton: Princeton University Press, 1994.

Tommasini, Anthony. *Virgil Thomson: composer on the aisle.* New York: W.W. Norton, 1997.

Tortelier, Paul. *A self-portrait: in conversation with David Blum.* London: Heinemann, 1984.

Tovey, Donald Francis. *A Companion to Beethoven's Pianoforte Sonatas.* Revised by Barry Cooper. London: The Associated Board, [1931], 1998.

Tovey, Donald Francis. *Beethoven.* London: Oxford University Press, 1944.

Tovey, Donald Francis. *Essays and lectures on music.* London: Oxford University Press, 1949.

Tovey, Donald Francis. *Essays in musical analysis.* London: Oxford University Press, H. Milford, 7 Vols., 1935—41.

Tovey, Donald Francis. *The forms of music: musical articles from The Encyclopaedia Britannica.* London: Oxford University Press, 1944.

Toye, Francis. *Giuseppe Verdi: his life and works.* London: William Heinemann Ltd., 1931.

Truscott, Harold. *Beethoven's late string quartets.* London: Dobson, 1968.

Tyler, William R. *The letters of Franz Liszt to Olga von Meyendorff, 1871—1886, in the Mildred Bliss Collection at Dumbarton Oaks.* Translated by William R. Tyler. Washington: Dumbarton Oaks, Trustees for Harvard University; Cambridge, Massachusetts: distributed by Harvard University Press, 1979.

Tyrrell, John. *Janáček: years of a life. Vol. 1, (1854—1914) The lonely blackbird.* London: Faber and Faber, 2006.

Tyrrell, John, Editor and Translator. *My life with Janáček: the memoirs of Zdenka Janácková.* London: Faber and Faber, 1998.

Tyson, Alan, Editor. *Beethoven studies 2.* Cambridge: Cambridge University Press, 1977.

Tyson, Alan, Editor. *Beethoven studies 3.* Cambridge: Cambridge University Press, 1982.

Tyson, Alan. *Mozart: studies of the autograph scores.* Cambridge, Massachusetts; London: Harvard University Press, 1987.

Tyson, Alan. *The authentic English editions of Beethoven.* London: Faber and Faber, 1963.

Underwood, J. A., Editor. *Gabriel Fauré: his life through his letters.* London: Marion Boyars, 1984.

Vechten, Carl van, Editor. *Nikolay, Rimsky-Korsakov: My musical life*. London: Martin Secker & Warburg Ltd., 1942.

Vinton, John. *Essays after a dictionary: music and culture at the close of Western civilization*. Lewisburg: Bucknell University Press, 1977.

Volkov, Solomon, Editor. *Testimony: the memoirs of Dmitri Shostakovich*. London: Faber and Faber, 1981.

Volta, Ornella, Editor. *A mammal's notebook: collected writings of Erik Satie*. London: Atlas Press, 1996.

Wagner, Richard. Beethoven: *With [a] supplement from the philosophical works of A. Schopenhauer*. Translated by E. Dannreuther. London: Reeves, 1893.

Wagner, Richard. *My life*. London: Constable and Company Ltd., 1911.

Walden, Valerie. *One hundred years of violoncello: a history of technique and performance practice, 1740–1840*. Cambridge: Cambridge University Press, 1998.

Walker, Alan. *Franz Liszt. Volume 1, The virtuoso years: 1811–1847*. New York: Alfred A. Knopf, 1983.

Walker, Alan. *Franz Liszt. Volume 2, The Weimar years: 1848–1861*. London: Faber and Faber, 1989.

Walker, Alan. *Franz Liszt. Volume 3, The final years, 1861–1886*. London: Faber and Faber, 1997.

Walker, Bettina. *My musical experiences*. London: Richard Bentley and Son, 1890.

Walker, Ernest. *Free thought and the musician, and other essays*. London; New York: Oxford University Press, 1946.

Walker, Frank. *Hugo Wolf: a biography*. London: J. M. Dent, 1951.

Walker, Frank. *The man Verdi*. London: Dent, 1962.

Wallace, Grace, *[Lady Wallace]. Beethoven's letters (1790–1826): from the collection of Dr. Ludwig Nohl . Also his letters to the Archduke Rudolph, Cardinal-Archbishop of Olmutz, K.W., from the collection of Dr. Ludwig Ritter Von Koĉhel*. London: Longmans, Green, 2 Vols., 1866.

Wallace, Robin. *Beethoven's critics: aesthetic dilemmas and resolutions during the composer's lifetime*. Cambridge; New York: Cambridge University Press, 1986.

Walter, Bruno. *Theme and variations: an autobiography*. London: H. Hamilton, 1948.

Warrack, John Hamilton. *Writings on music*. Cambridge: Cambridge University Press, 1981.

Wasielewski, Wilhelm Joseph von. *Life of Robert Schumann: with letters, 1833–1852*. London: William Reeves, 1878.

Watkins, Glenn. *Proof through the night: music and the Great War*. Berkeley: University of California Press, 2003.

Watkins, Glenn. *Pyramids at the Louvre: music, culture, and collage from Stravinsky to the postmodernists*. Cambridge, Massachusetts; London: Belknap Press of Harvard University Press, 1994.

Watkins, Glenn. *Soundings: music in the twentieth century*. New York: Schirmer Books London: Collier Macmillan, 1988.

Watson, Derek. *Liszt*. London: J. M. Dent, 1989.

Weaver, William, Editor. *The Verdi-Boito correspondence*. Chicago; London: University of Chicago Press, 1994.

Wegeler, Franz. *Remembering Beethoven: the biographical notes of Franz Wegeler and Ferdinand Ries*. London: Andre Deutsch, 1988.

Weingartner, Felix. *Buffets and rewards: a musician's reminiscences*. London: Hutchinson & Co., 1937.

Weinstock, Herbert. *Rossini: a biography*. New York: Limelight, 1987.

Weiss, Piero and Richard Taruskin. *Music in the Western World: a history in documents*. New York: Schirmer; London: Collier Macmillan, 1984.

Weissweiler, Eva *The complete correspondence of Clara and Robert Schumann*. New York: Peter Lang, 2 Vols., 1994.

Whittaker, William Gillies. *Collected essays*. London: Oxford University Press, 1940.

Whittall, Arnold. *Exploring twentieth-century music: tradition and innovation*. Cambridge; New York: Cambridge University Press, 2003.

Whittall, Arnold. *Music since the First World War*. London: J. M. Dent, 1977.

Whitton, Kenneth S. *Lieder: an introduction to German song*. London: Julia MacRae, 1984.

Wightman, Alistair, Editor. *Szymanowski on music: selected writings of Karol Szymanowski*. London: Toccata Press, 1999.

Wilhelm, Kurt. *Richard Strauss: an intimate portrait*. London: Thames and Hudson, 1999.

Will, Richard James. *The characteristic symphony in the age of Haydn and Beethoven*. Cambridge: Cambridge University Press, 2002.

Willetts, Pamela J. *Beethoven and England: an account of sources in the British Museum*. London: British Museum, 1970.

Williams, Adrian, Editor and Translator. *Liszt, Franz: Selected letters*. Oxford: Clarendon Press, 1998.

Williams, Adrian. *Portrait of Liszt: by himself and his contemporaries*. Oxford: Clarendon Press, 1990.

Williams, Ralph Vaughan. *Heirs and rebels: letters written to each other and occasional writings on music*. London; New York: Oxford University Press, 1959.

Williams, Ralph Vaughan. *Some thoughts on Beethoven's Choral symphony: with writings on other musical subjects*. London; Oxford University Press, 1953.

Williams, Ralph Vaughan. *The making of music*. Ithaca, New York: Cornell University Press, 1955.

Williams, Ursula Vaughan. *R.V.W.: a biography of Ralph Vaughan Williams*. London: Oxford University Press, 1964.

Wilson, Conrad. *Notes on Beethoven: 20 crucial works*. Edinburgh: Saint Andrew Press, 2003.

Wilson, Elizabeth. *Shostakovich: a life remembered*. Princeton, New Jersey: Princeton University Press, 1994.

Winter, Robert, Editor. *Beethoven, performers, and critics: the Inter-*

national Beethoven Congress, Detroit, 1977. Detroit: Wayne State University Press, 1980.

Winter, Robert. *Compositional origins of Beethoven's opus 131.* Ann Arbor, Michigan: UMI Research Press, 1982.

Winter, Robert and Robert Martin, Editors. *The Beethoven quartet companion.* Berkeley: University of California Press, 1994.

Wolf, Eugene K. and Edward H. Roesner, Editors. *Studies in musical sources and style: essays in honor of Jan LaRue.* Madison, Wisconsin: A-R Editions, 1990.

Wolff, Christoph and Robert Riggs. *The string quartets of Haydn, Mozart and Beethoven: studies of the autograph manuscripts: a conference at Isham Memorial Library, March 15–17, 1979.* Cambridge, Massachusetts: Department of Music, Harvard University, 1980.

Wolff, Konrad. *Masters of the keyboard: individual style elements in the piano music of Bach, Haydn, Mozart, Beethoven, Schubert, Chopin, and Brahms.* Bloomington: Indiana University Press, 1990.

Wörner, Karl Heinrich. *Stockhausen: life and work.* London: Faber, 1973.

Wright, Donald, Editor. *Cardus on music: a centenary collection.* London: Hamish Hamilton, 1988.

Wyndham, Henry Saxe. *August Manns and the Saturday concerts: a memoir and a retrospect.* London and Felling-on-Tyne, New York, The Walter Scott Publishing Co., Ltd., 1909.

Yastrebtsev, V.V. Edited and Translated by Florence Jonas. *Reminiscences of Rimsky-Korsakov.* New York: Columbia University Press, 1985.

Yates, Peter. *Twentieth century music: its evolution from the end of the harmonic era into the present era of sound.* London: Allen & Unwin Ltd., 1968.

Young, Percy M. *Beethoven: a Victorian tribute based on the papers of Sir George Smart.* London: D. Dobson, 1976.

Young, Percy M. *George Grove, 1820–1900: a biography.* London: Macmillan, 1980.

Young, Percy M. *Letters of Edward Elgar and other writings.* London: Geoffrey Bles, 1956.

Young, Percy M., Editor. *Letters to Nimrod: Edward Elgar to August Jaeger, 1897–1908.* London: Dennis Dobson, 1965.

Young, Percy M. *The concert tradition: from the middle ages to the twentieth century.* London: Routledge and Kegan Paul, 1965.

Young, Rob, Editor. *(Brief Description): Undercurrents: the hidden wiring of modern music.* London; New York, N.Y.: Continuum, 2002.

Yourke, Electra Slonimsky, Editor. *Nicolas Slonimsky: writings on music.* New York, N.Y.; London: Routledge, 4 Vols. 2003-2005.

Slonimsky, Nicolas. *The great composers and their works.* Edited by Electra Slonimsky Yourke. New York: Schirmer Books, 2 Vols. 2000.

Ysaÿe, Antoine. *Ysaÿe: his life, work and influence.* London: W. Heinemann, 1947.

Zamoyski, Adam. *Paderewski.*

London: Collins, 1982.

Zegers, Mirjam, Editor. *Louis Andriessen: The art of stealing time.* Todmorden: Arc Music, 2002.

Zemanova, Mirka, Editor. *Janácek's uncollected essays on music.* London: Marion Boyars, 1989.

INDEX

Allgemeine musikalische Zeitung (*AmZ*) X, 2-3, 5-6
Antheil, George 7, 140
Arrau, Claudio 8-10, 153
Barenboim, Daniel 10-11, 141
Barford, Philip 11-12
Bartók, Béla 12, 146, 150, 159
Bekker, Paul XIII, 12-13, 141
Berlioz, Hector XII, 13-16, 55, 64, 141, 144, 146, 157, 160
Bliss, Arthur 16-17, 141, 164, 169
Bloch, Ernst XII, 17-18, 141
Blom, Eric XIV, 18, 19, 125, 142, 164
Brendel, Alfred XIII, XVII, 19-22, 83, 111-112, 143
Britten, Benjamin 22-23, 154, 159
Bülow, Hans von XI, 23-24, 45, 59, 93, 122, 137
Busoni, Ferruccio 24, 26, 115, 130, 141, 144
Carter, Elliot 26-27, 141, 147, 168
Cockshot, John V. 27

Cooper, Martin VI, 27-28, 111, 145, 155
Czerny, Carl I, XIV, 25, 28-33, 44, 45, 57-58, 61-62, 65, 72, 84, 87, 104, 140, 147
D'Indy, Vincent 54-55, 75, 169
Dahlhaus, Carl 33, 146
Debussy, Claude 12, 34, 49, 143, 146, 152, 153, 156, 157, 161, 167
Dvořák, Antonín XII, 34-35, 147
Dyson, George XII, 35-36, 147
Einstein, Alfred 36-37, 39, 147
Elterlein, Ernst von XI, 37-40, 148
Ertmann, Dorothea von 40, 42
Ferneyhough, Brian 42-43, 142
Fischer, Edwin XIII, 43-47, 65, 149
Godowsky, Leopold 47-48, 160
Gordon, Stewart 48-49, 150
Grainger, Percy 49, 147, 150
Hallé, Sir Charles II, 50-53, 151, 154, 163
Hoffman, E. T. A XIII, 53-54

Kinderman, William XIII, 56-57, 154
Landon, H. C. Robbins 7, 57, 61, 155-156
Leschetizky, Theodor 57-58, 153
Liszt, Franz 8, 14-16, 25, 45, 50, 58-68, 93, 116, 118, 133-134, 140, 153, 156, 158, 164, 167, 169-171
Lutoslovwski, Witold 68-69
MacDowell, Edward XII, 69, 156, 157
Mahler, Gustav 24, 70, 136, 141, 150, 157-158
Matthews, Dennis 70, 72-73, 158
Mellers, Wilfrid 74, 105, 152, 158, 162
Messian, Olivier 74-75, 158
Newman, William S. 59, 63, 75, 103, 104, 160
Nielsen, Carl 75-76, 159, 161
Parry, Sir Hubert 76-78, 147, 150
Pressler, Menahan 78
Prokofiev, Sergei 79-80, 151, 162-164
Richter, Sviatoslav 81, 149
Ries, Ferdinand 82-85, 128, 171
Rolland, Romain XII, 86, 164
Rosen, Charles 87-92, 164
Rubinstein, Anton 70, 92-95, 137
Rubinstein, Arthur 95-97, 110, 111, 130, 164
Russell, Sir John VIII, XVI, 97, 176
Rye, Matthew 98, 164

Saint-Saëns, Camille 98-100, 151, 163, 165
Schindler, Anton Felix XI, 7, 27, 41, 42, 100-104, 106, 119, 165
Schnabel, Artur XII, 37, 87, 106-114, 165
Schoenberg, Arnold 115, 120, 136, 140, 143, 160, 167-168
Schonberg, Harold Charles 59, 84, 93, 95, 98, 106, 115-116, 165
Schumann, Clara 60, 91, 117-118, 144, 156, 157, 160, 171
Scriabin, Alexander 120-121, 142
Serkin, Peter 121
Shedlock, John 121-122, 166
Sloboda, John 123
Stokowski, Leopold 124, 144
Stravinsky, Igor 77, 124-126, 132, 146, 148, 153, 168, 171
Tchaikovsky, Peter 126-127, 149, 151, 161, 163, 169
Thayer, Alexander Wheelock 127-128, 169
Thomson, Virgil 110, 113-115, 129-130, 153, 155, 162, 169
Tovey, Donald Francis V, XIII, 130-131, 146, 169
Wagner, Richard XI, 89, 132-134, 137, 143, 148, 153, 156, 163, 170
Webern, Anton von 134-136, 140, 159, 163
Wolf, Hugo 136-137, 160, 162, 167, 170, 172

ABOUT THE AUTHOR

Terence M. Russell graduated with first class honours in architecture and was a nominee for the coveted Silver Medal of the Royal Institute of British Architects. He is a Fellow of the Royal Incorporation of Architects in Scotland (retired), was formerly Reader in the School of Arts, Culture and Environment at the University of Edinburgh, a Fellow of the British Higher Education Academy, and Senior Assessor to the Scottish Higher Education Funding Council. Alongside his professional work in the field of architecture – embracing practice, teaching and research – he has maintained a lifetime's interest in the music and musicology of Beethoven. He has an equal admiration for the work of Franz Schubert and was for many years an active member of the Schubert Institute, UK. His book writings in the field of architecture include the following:

The Built Environment: A Subject Index, Gregg Publishing (1989):
- Vol. 1: Town planning and urbanism, architecture, gardens and landscape design
- Vol. 2: Environmental technology, constructional engineering, building and materials
- Vol. 3: Decorative art and industrial design, international exhibitions and collections, recreational and performing arts
- Vol. 4: Public health, municipal services, community welfare

Architecture in the Encyclopédie of Diderot and D'Alemebert: The Letterpress Articles and Selected Engravings, Scolar Press (1993)

The Encyclopaedic Dictionary in the Eighteenth Century: Architecture, Arts and Crafts, Scolar Press (1997):
- Vol. 1: John Harris, Lexicon Technicum
- Vol. 2: Ephraim Chambers, Cyclopaedia
- Vol. 3: The Builder's Dictionary
- Vol. 4: Samuel Johnson, A Dictionary of the English Language
- Vol. 5: A Society of Gentlemen, Encyclopaedia Britannica

Gardens and Landscapes in the Encyclopédie of Diderot and D'Alemebert: The Letterpress Articles and Selected Engravings, 2 Vols., Ashgate (1999)

The Napoleonic Survey of Egypt: The Monuments and Customs of Egypt, 2 Vols., Ashgate (2001)

The Discovery of Egypt: Vivant Denon's Travels with Napoleon's Army, History Press (2005)

www.ingramcontent.com/pod-product-compliance
Lightning Source LLC
Chambersburg PA
CBHW011957090526
44590CB00023B/3762